100 MOST COMMON
CHINESE CHARACTERS
COLORING PAGES

Learn how to read Chinese characters simply by coloring! With crayons, markers, water colors or colored pencils you can create mini-posters of some of the most common words in the Chinese language! The tracing and coloring of each page will help you to become more familiar with each character and its distinctive shape and components.

These pages can be photo-copied and used for whole class lessons, small group instruction, independent learning or even for homework review.

Note that, as in English, many words in Chinese have more than one meaning. Occasionally a Chinese character can even have more than one pronunciation. We have included the Mandarin pronunciation of each Chinese word. Other dialects, such as Cantonese use the same written characters but pronounce the words very differently.

What is the best way to learn Chinese? Of course, the easiest way to learn a new language is to live in a country that speaks that language. This is not always possible, so here are some tips for those who are learning from home:

1. Watch television programs in Chinese. Many cable operators and streaming services, such as Netflix, offer a variety of programs in Chinese with English subtitles.

2. Watch videos online, such as on YouTube. You can slow down the speed of online videos and control the captions.

3. Download language-learning apps on your phone or tablet. Many are free!

4. Look for language partners online. Many will teach you their language in exchange for your help with their English.

5. Look for more of our reproducible Chinese language learning materials!

www.SpeakChineseToday.com

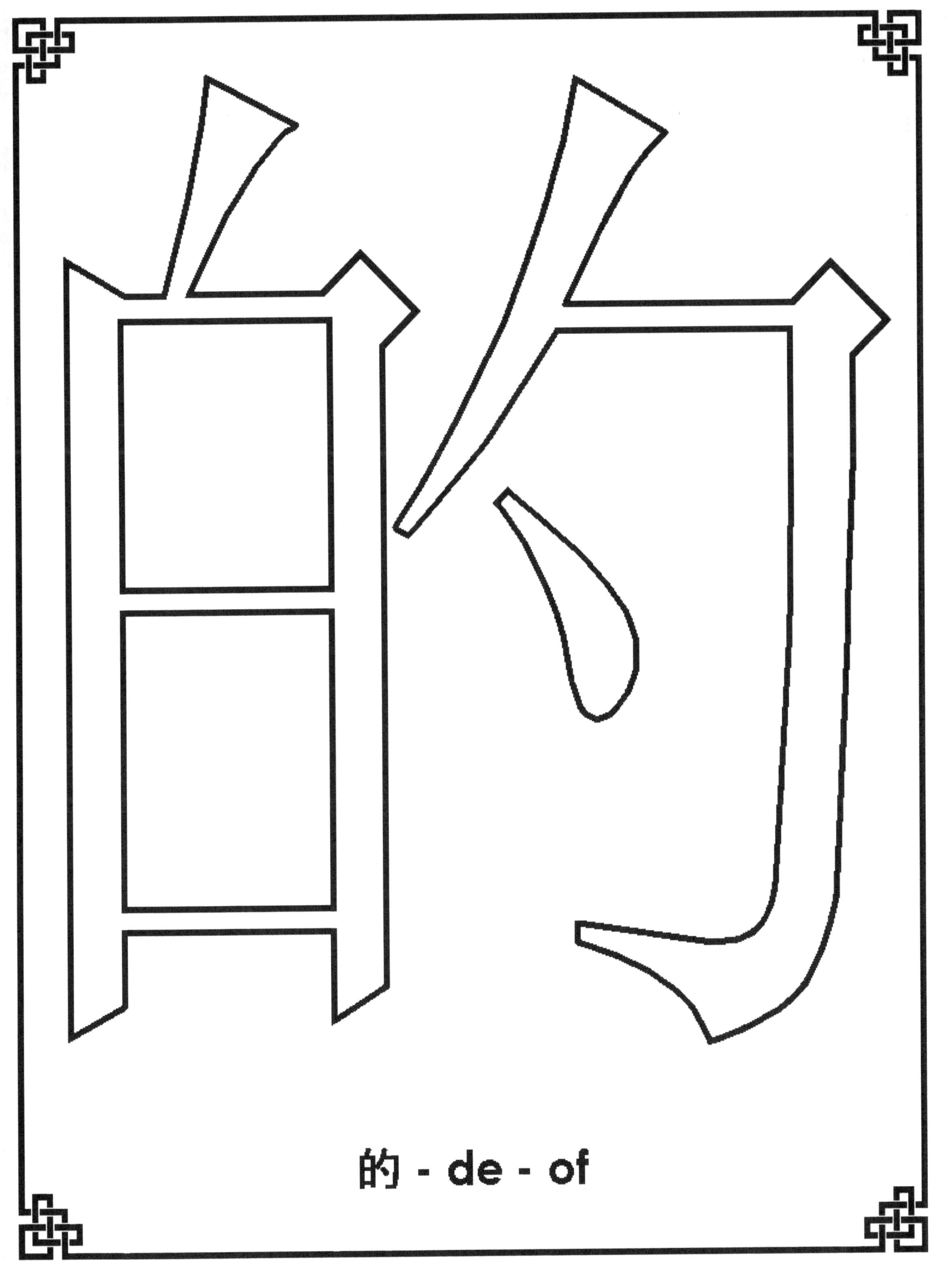

的 - de - of

一 - yī - one

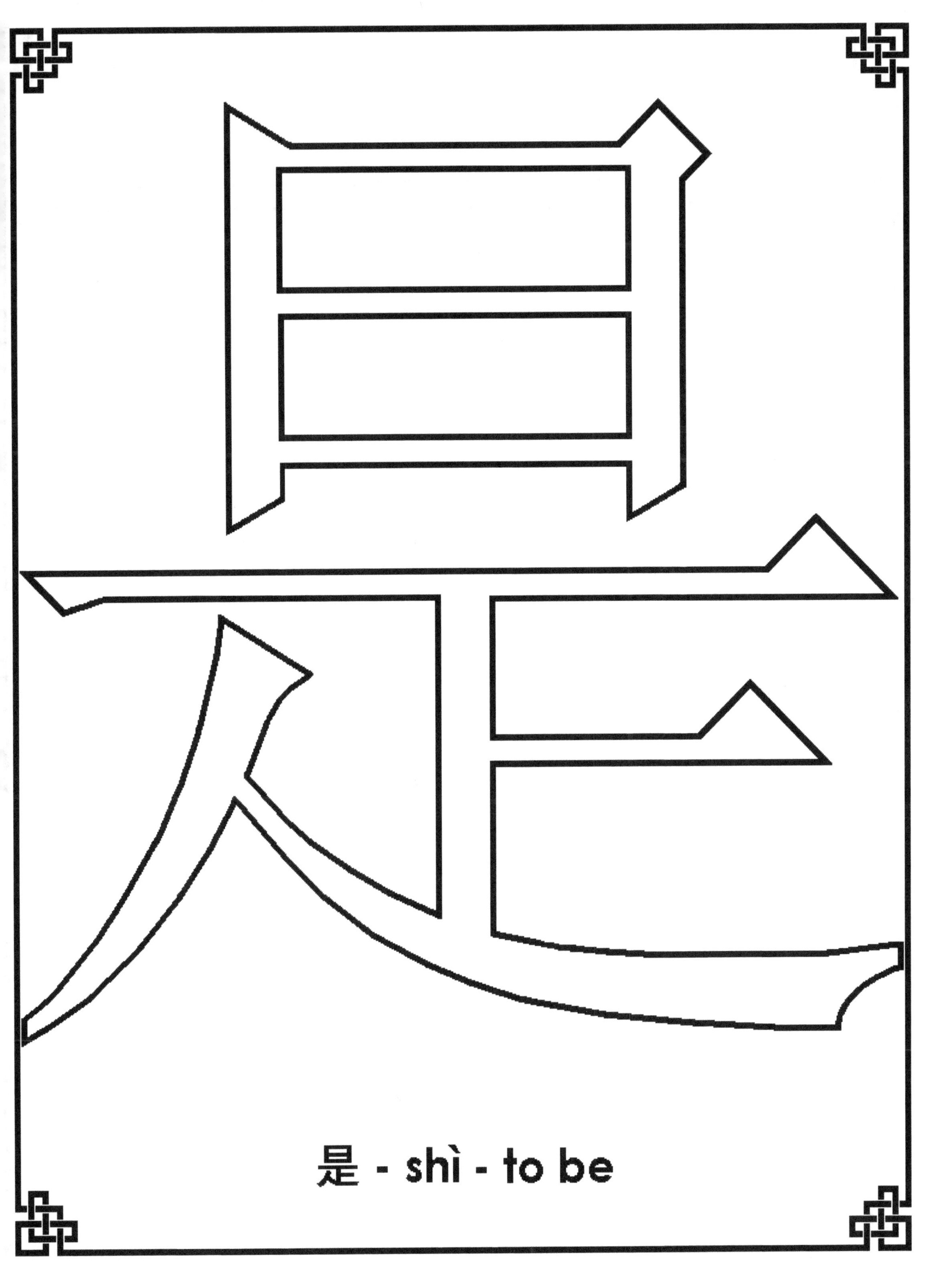

是 - shì - to be

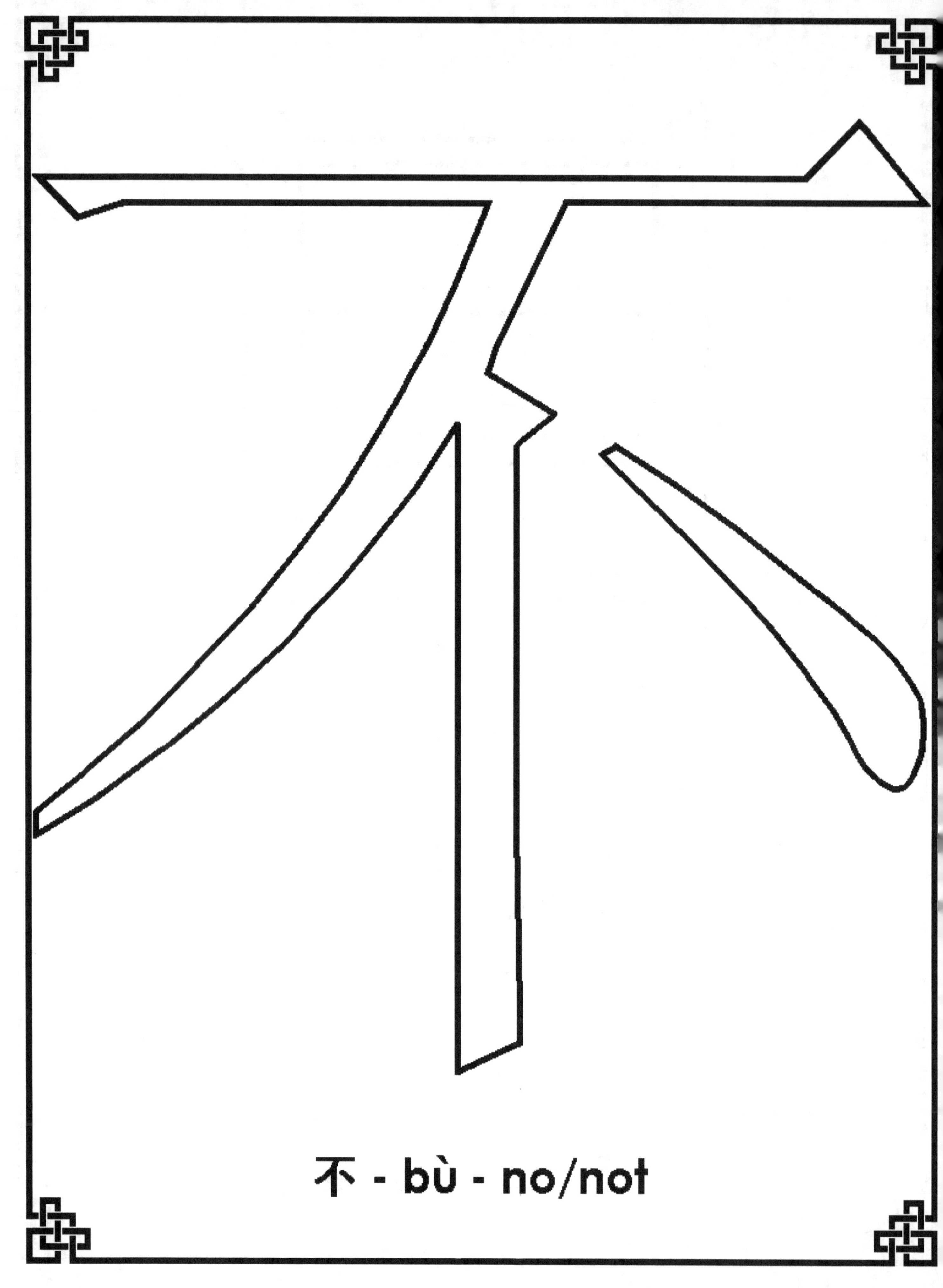

不 - bù - no/not

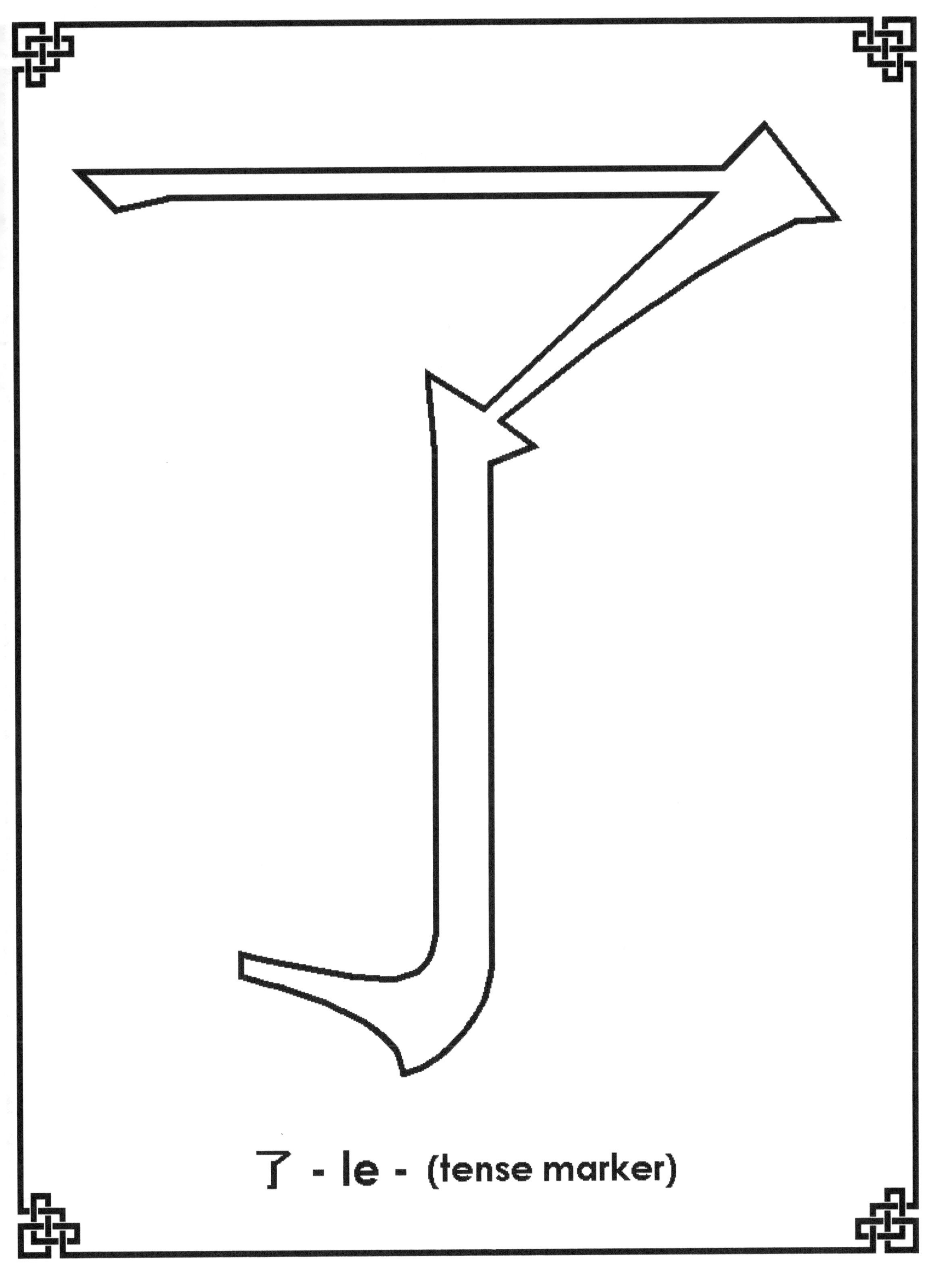

了 - le - (tense marker)

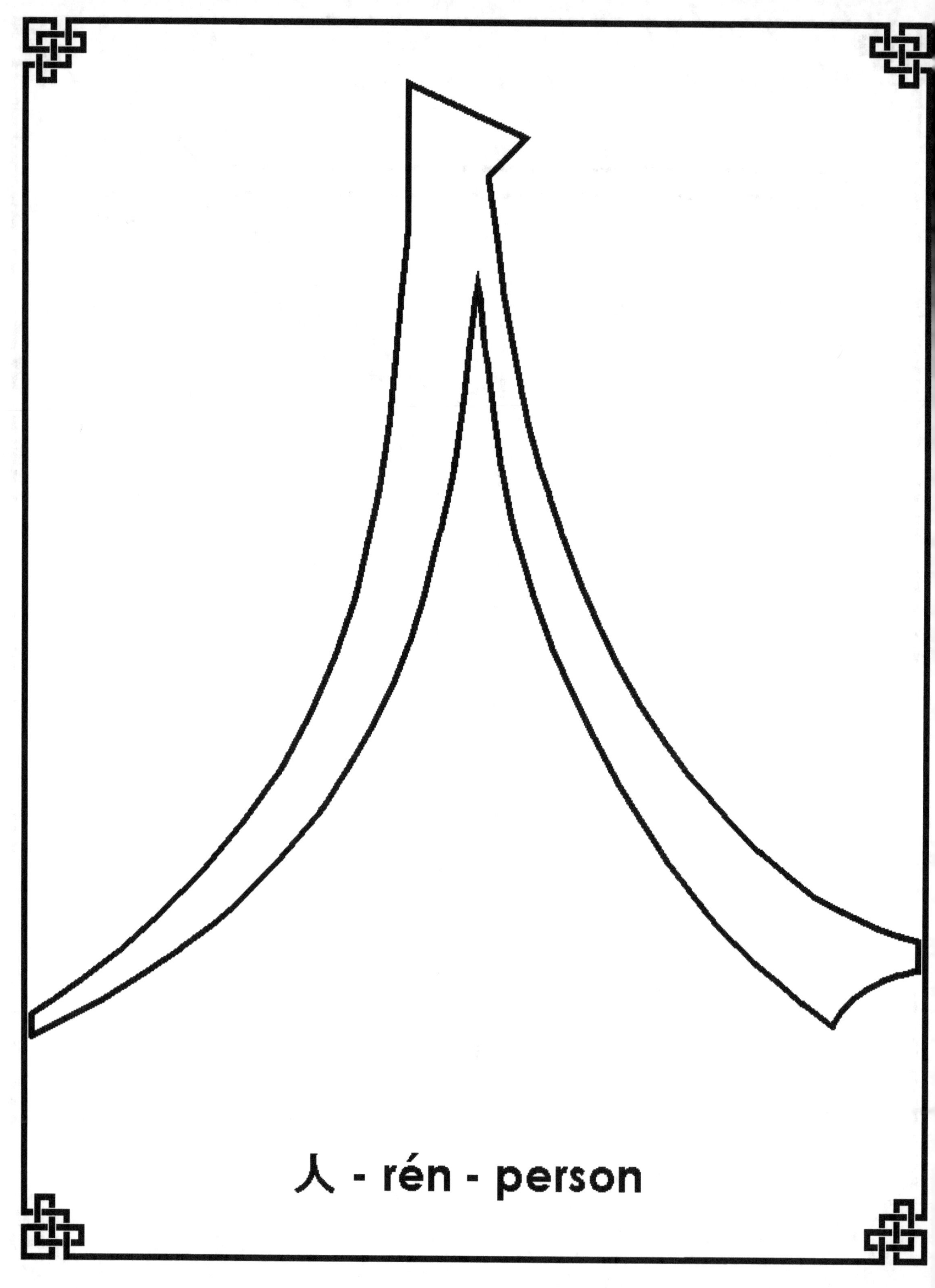

人 - rén - person

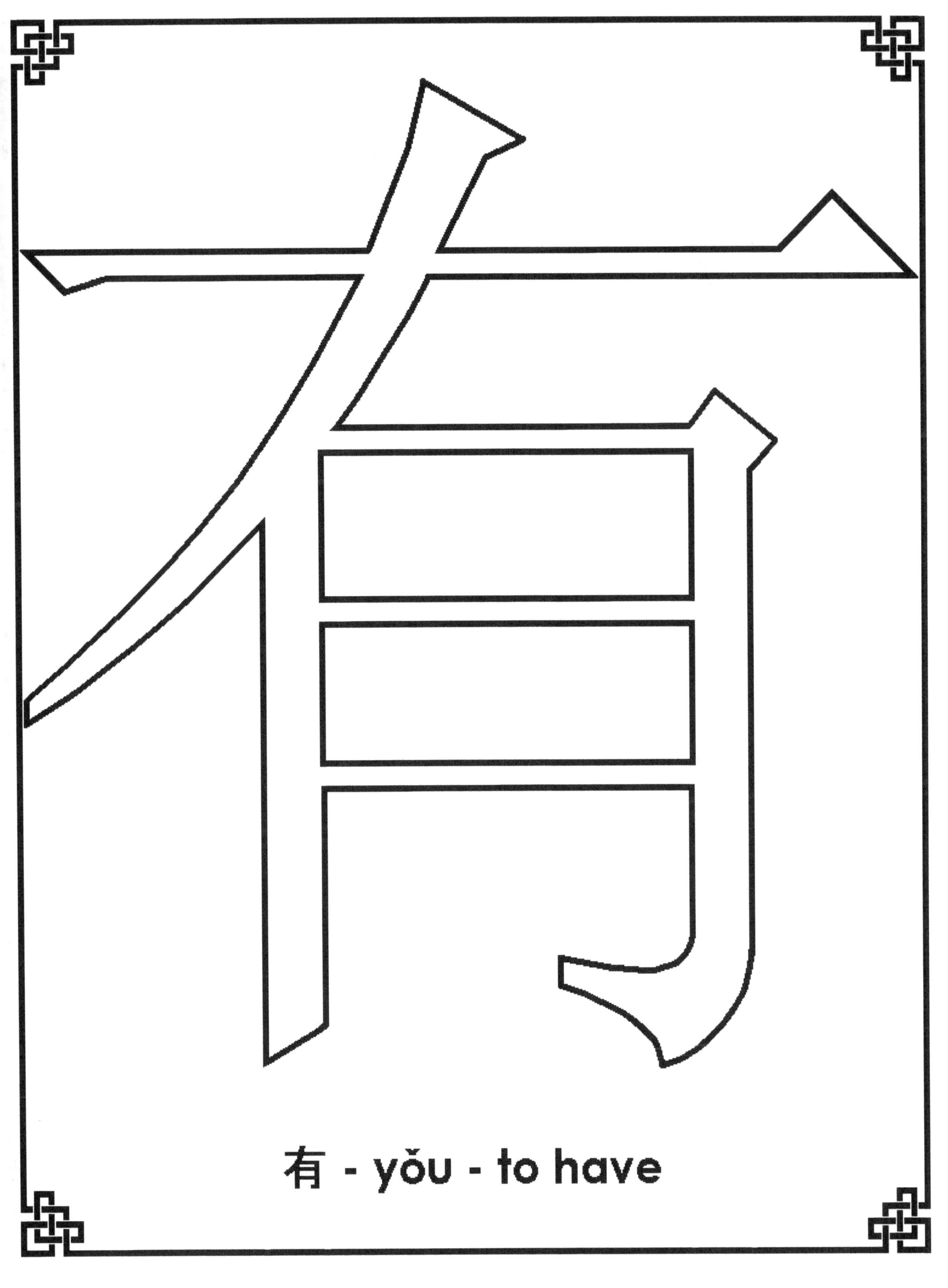

有 - yǒu - to have

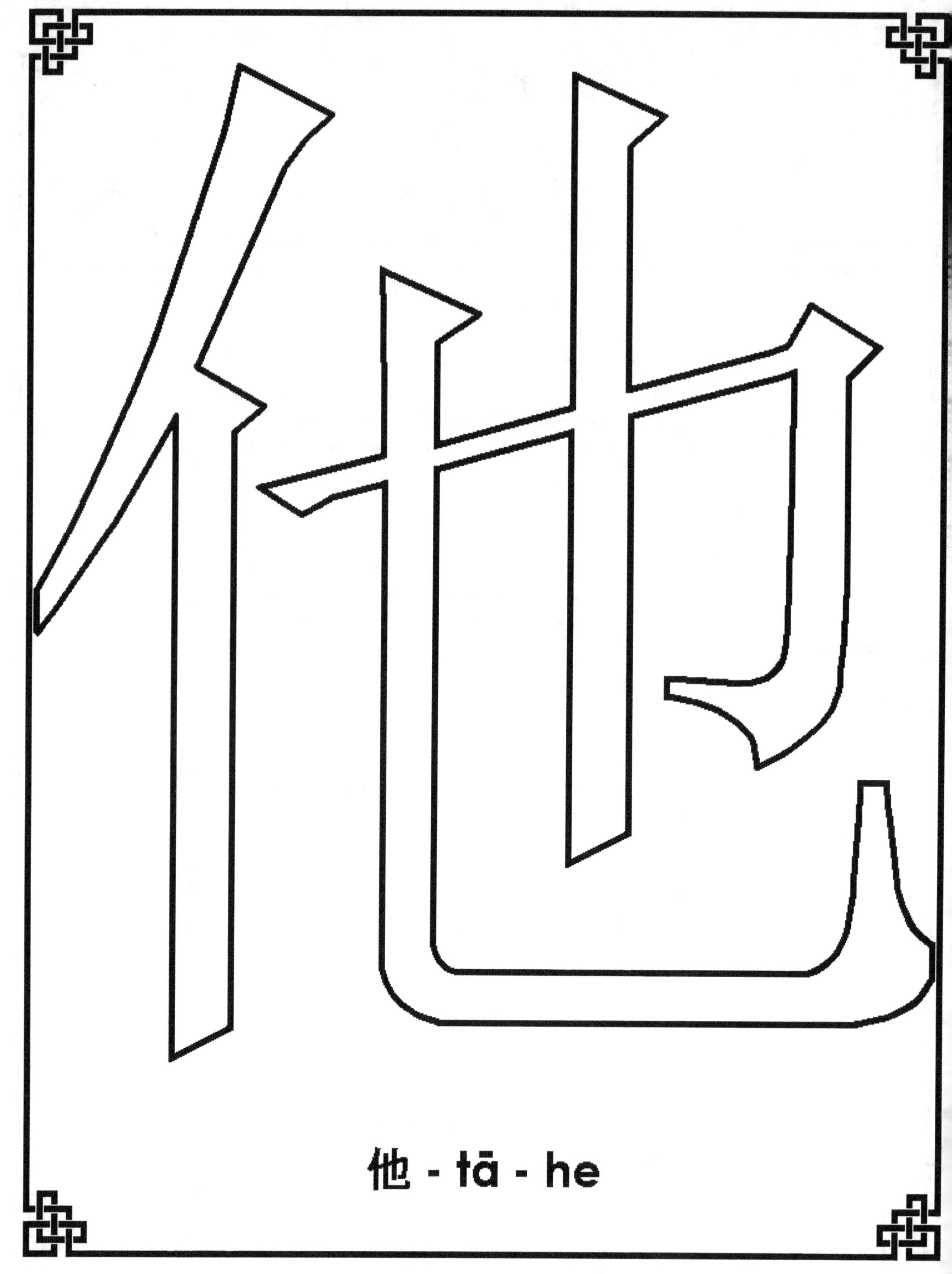

他 - tā - he

这 - zhè - this

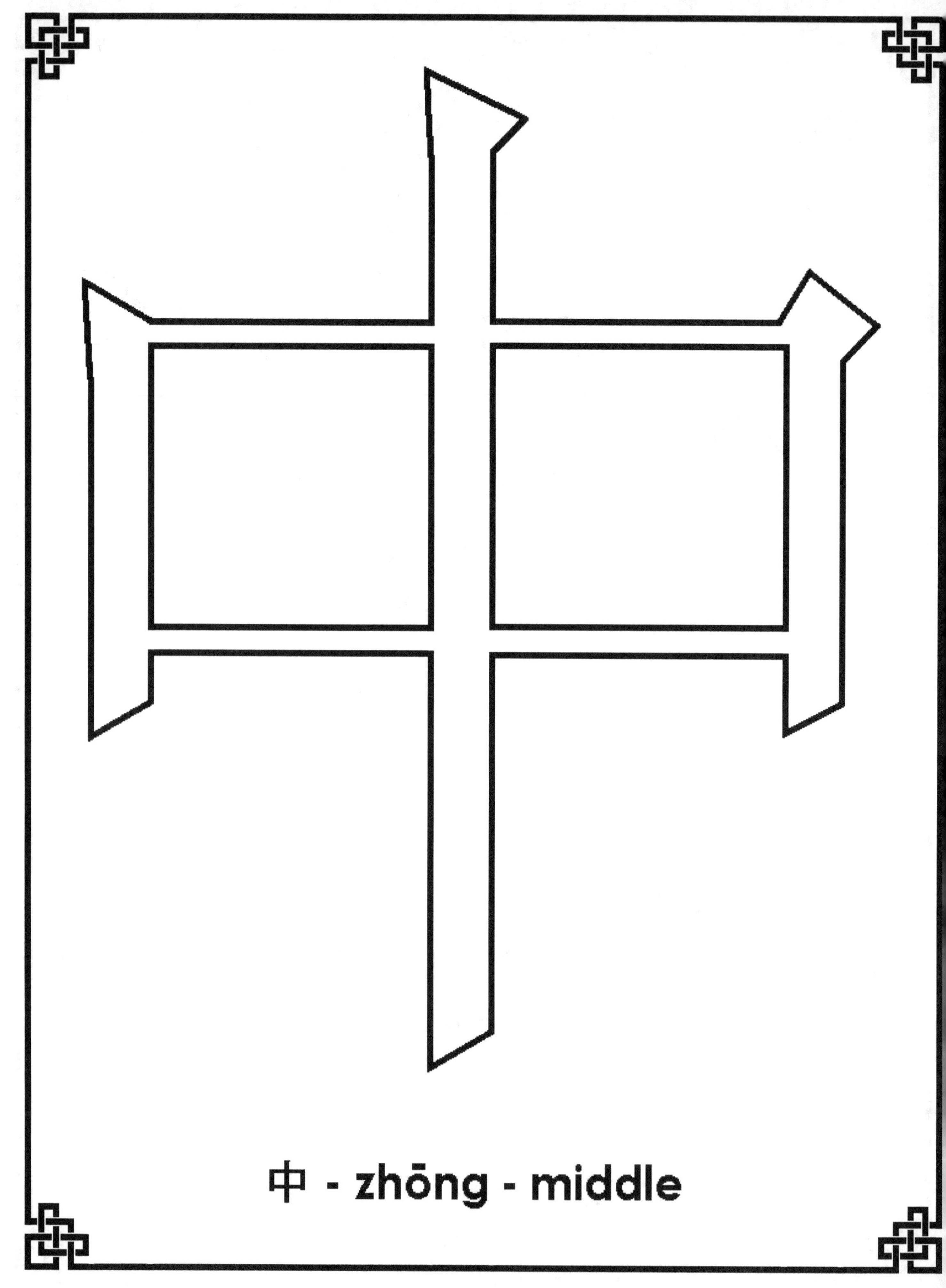

中 - zhōng - middle

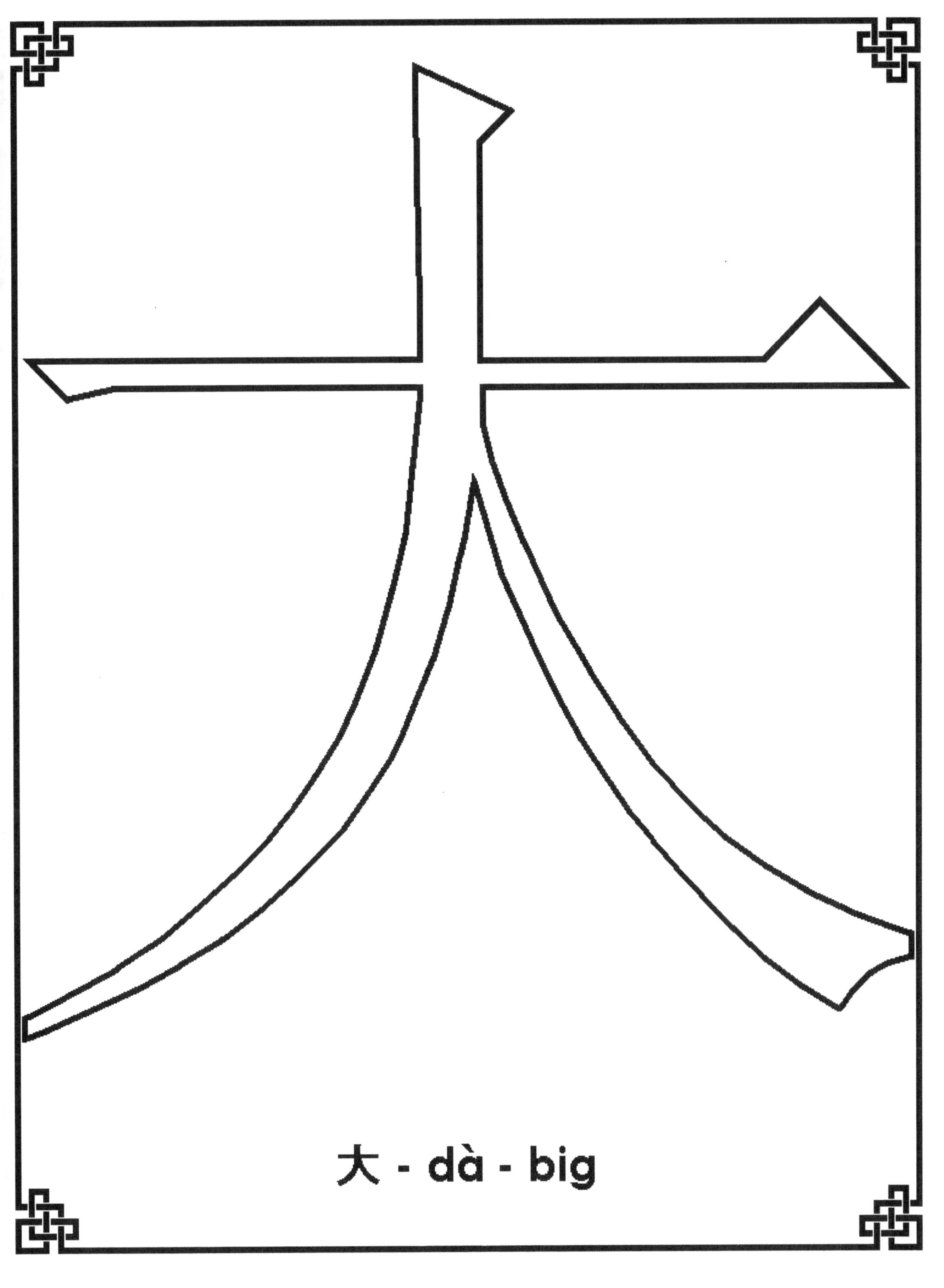

大 - dà - big

来 - lái - to come

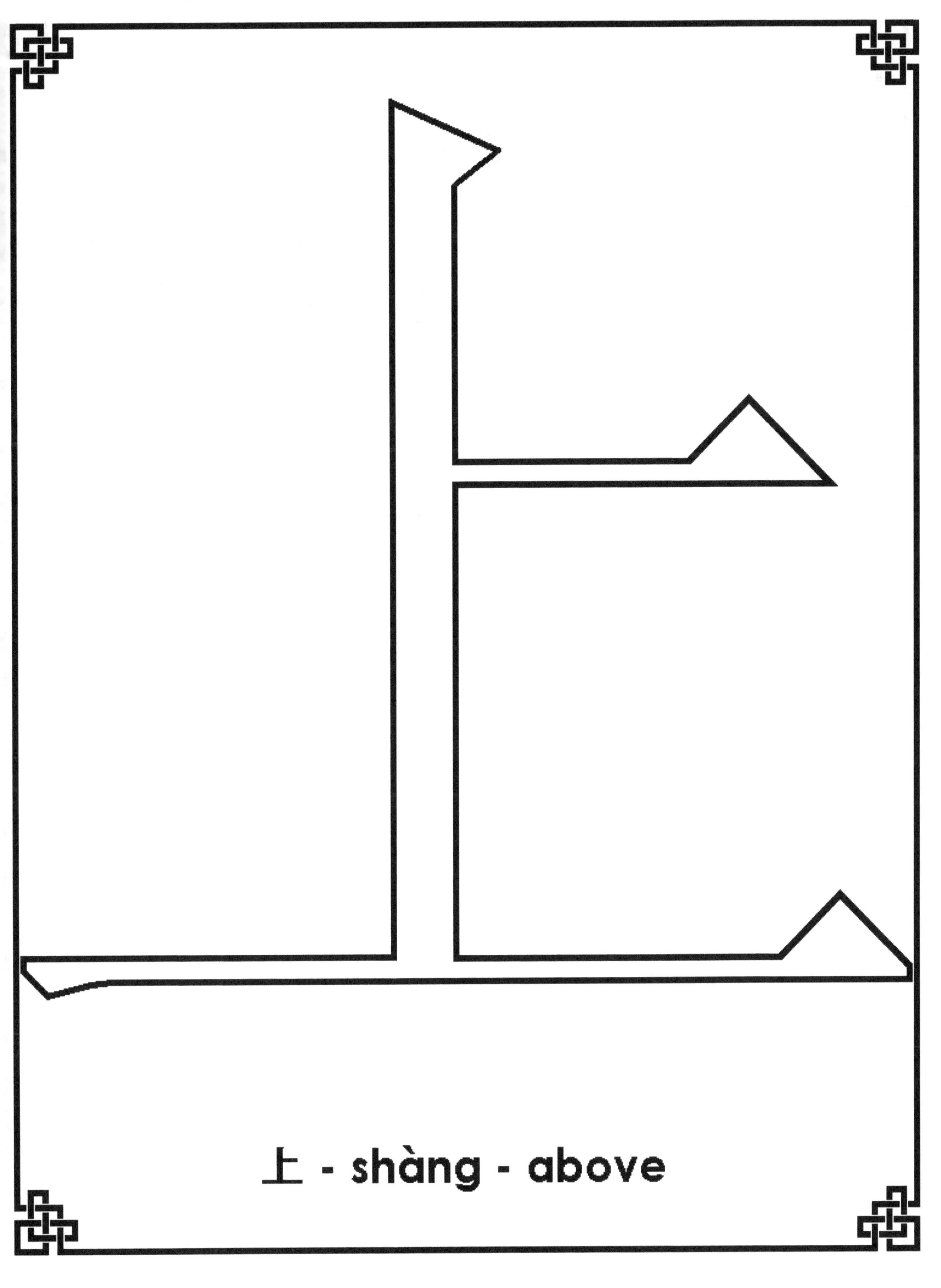

上 - shàng - above

国 - guó - country

个 - gè - (measure word)

到 - dào - arrive

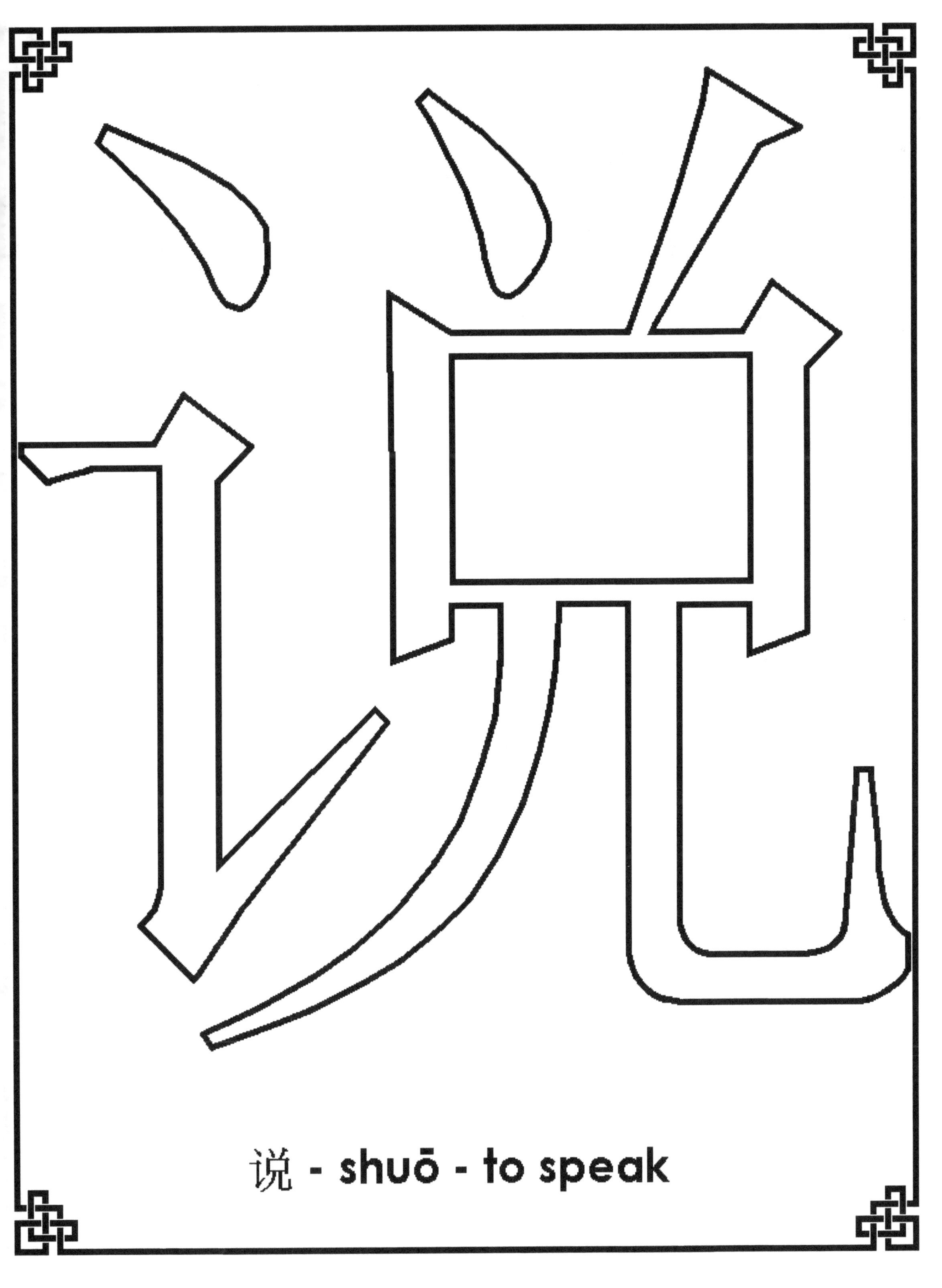

说 - shuō - to speak

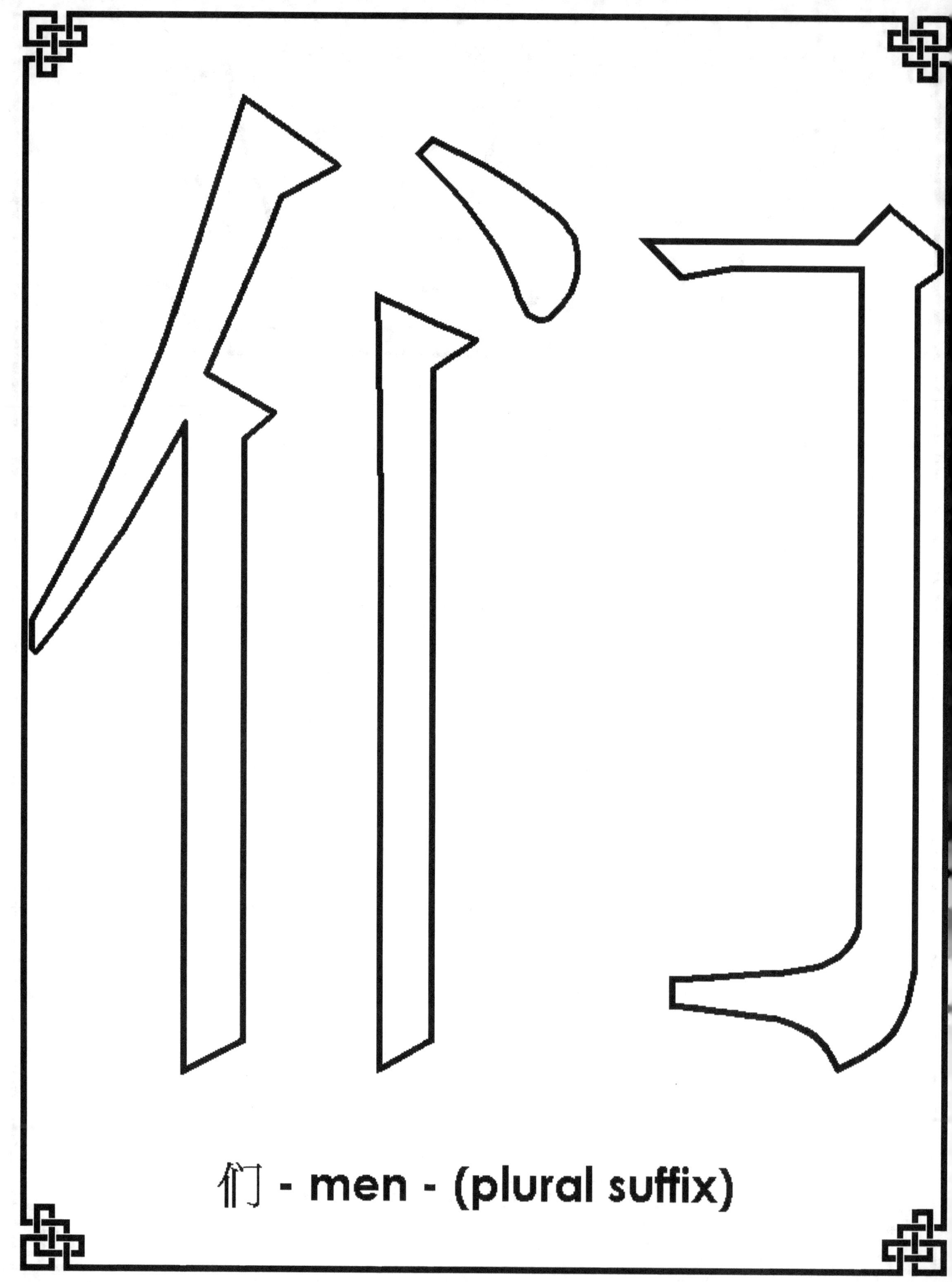

们 - men - (plural suffix)

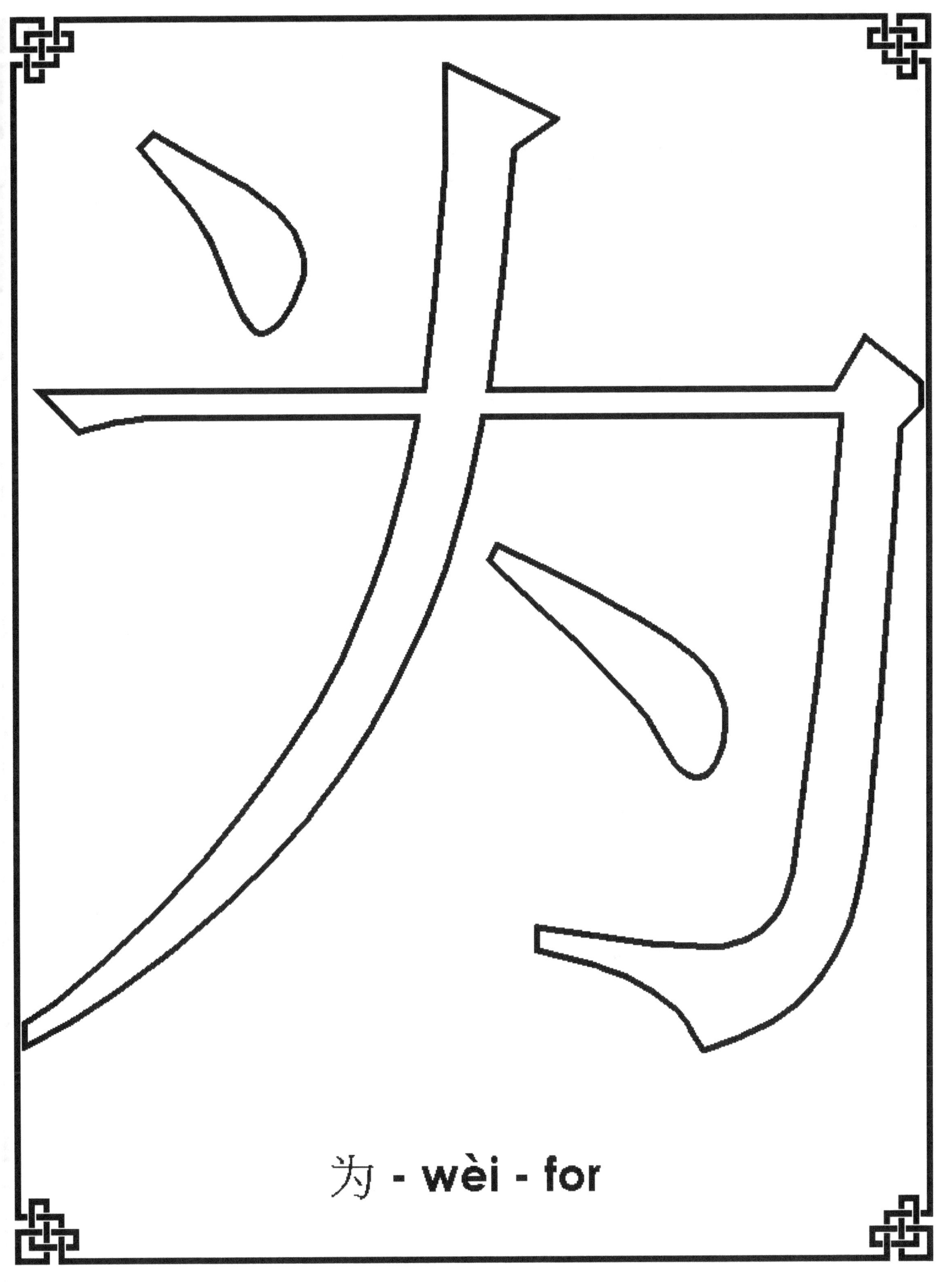

为 - wèi - for

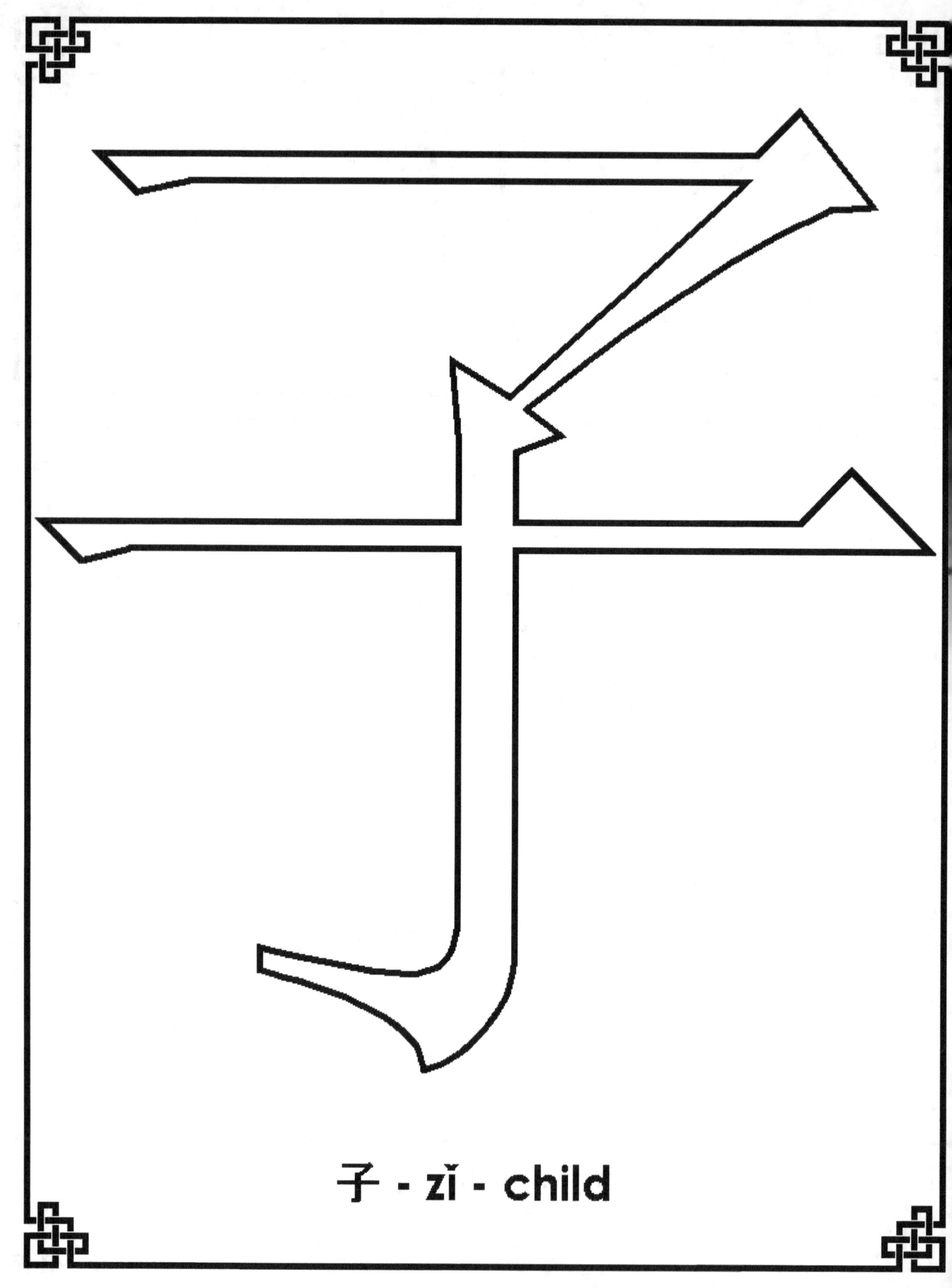

子 - zǐ - child

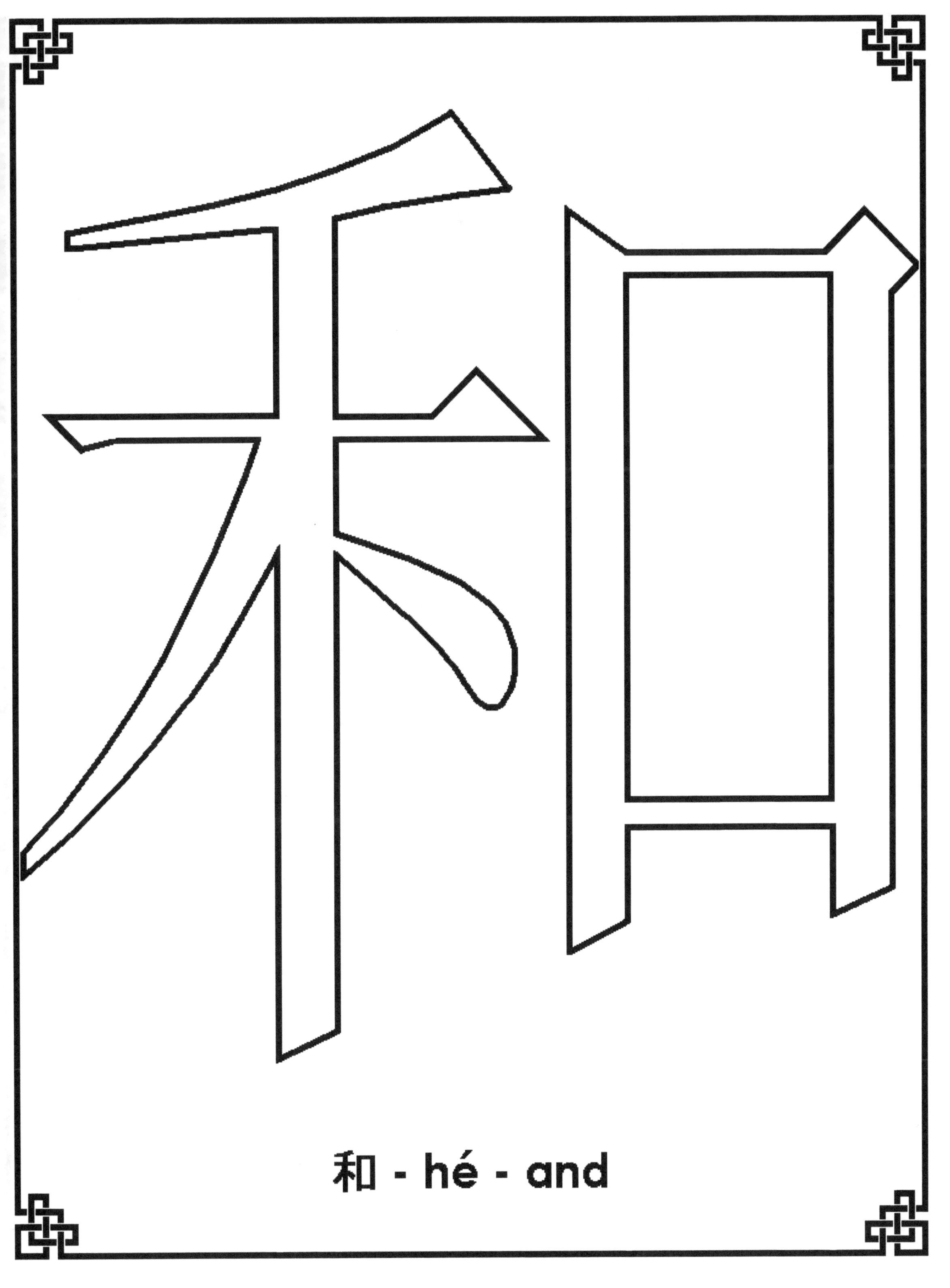

和 - hé - and

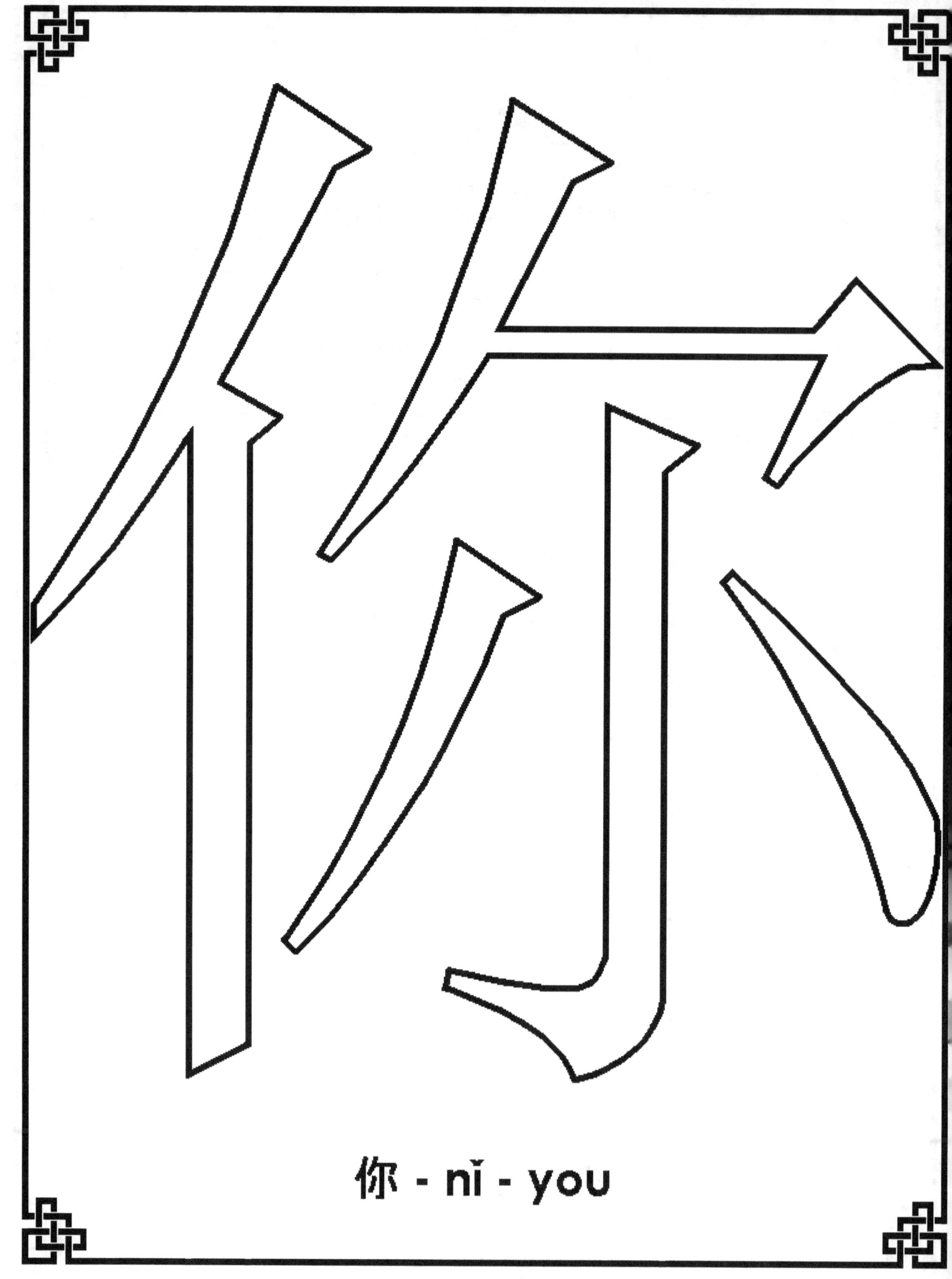

你 - nǐ - you

地 - dì - earth/ground

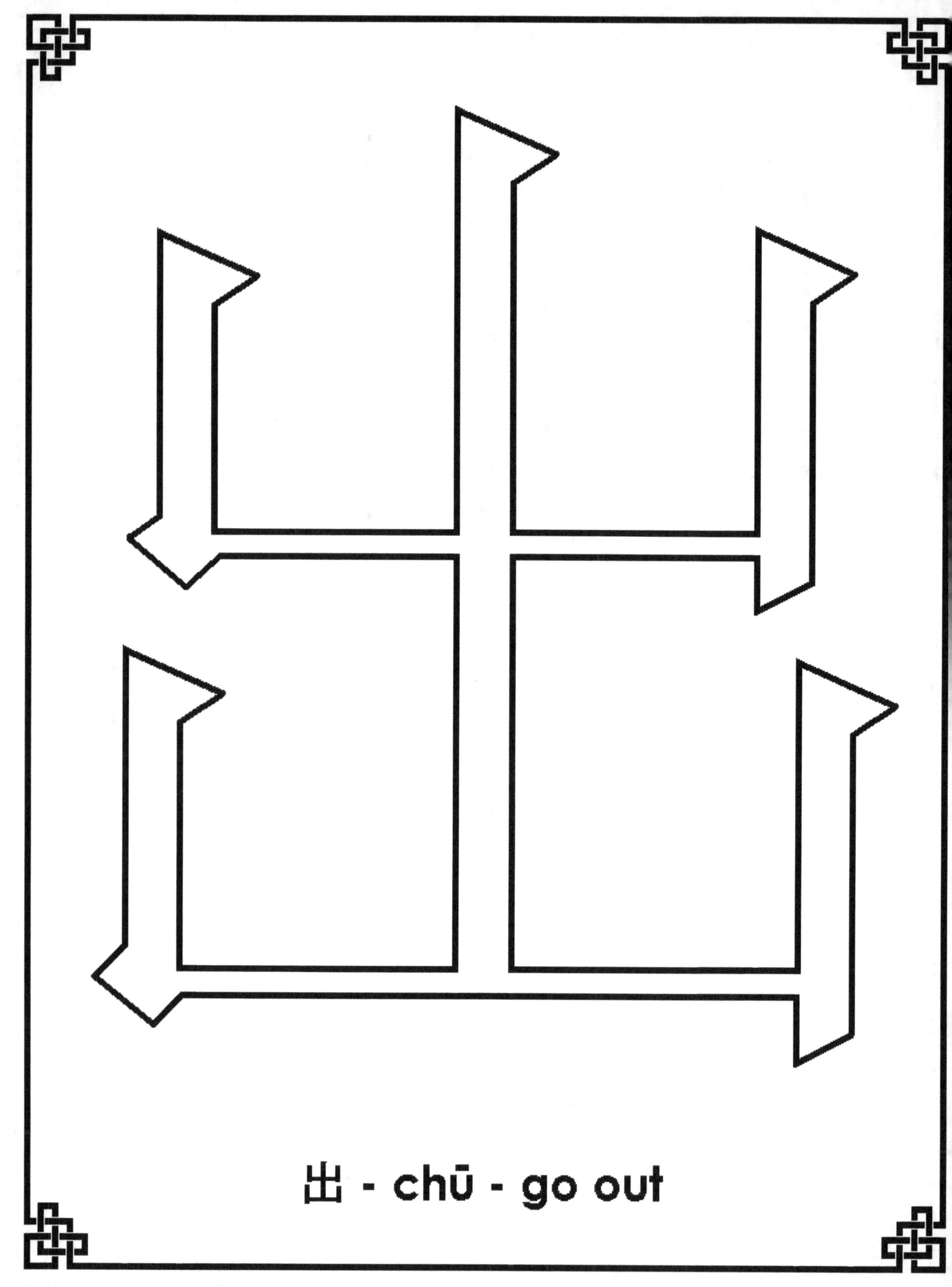

出 - chū - go out

道 - dào - way/path

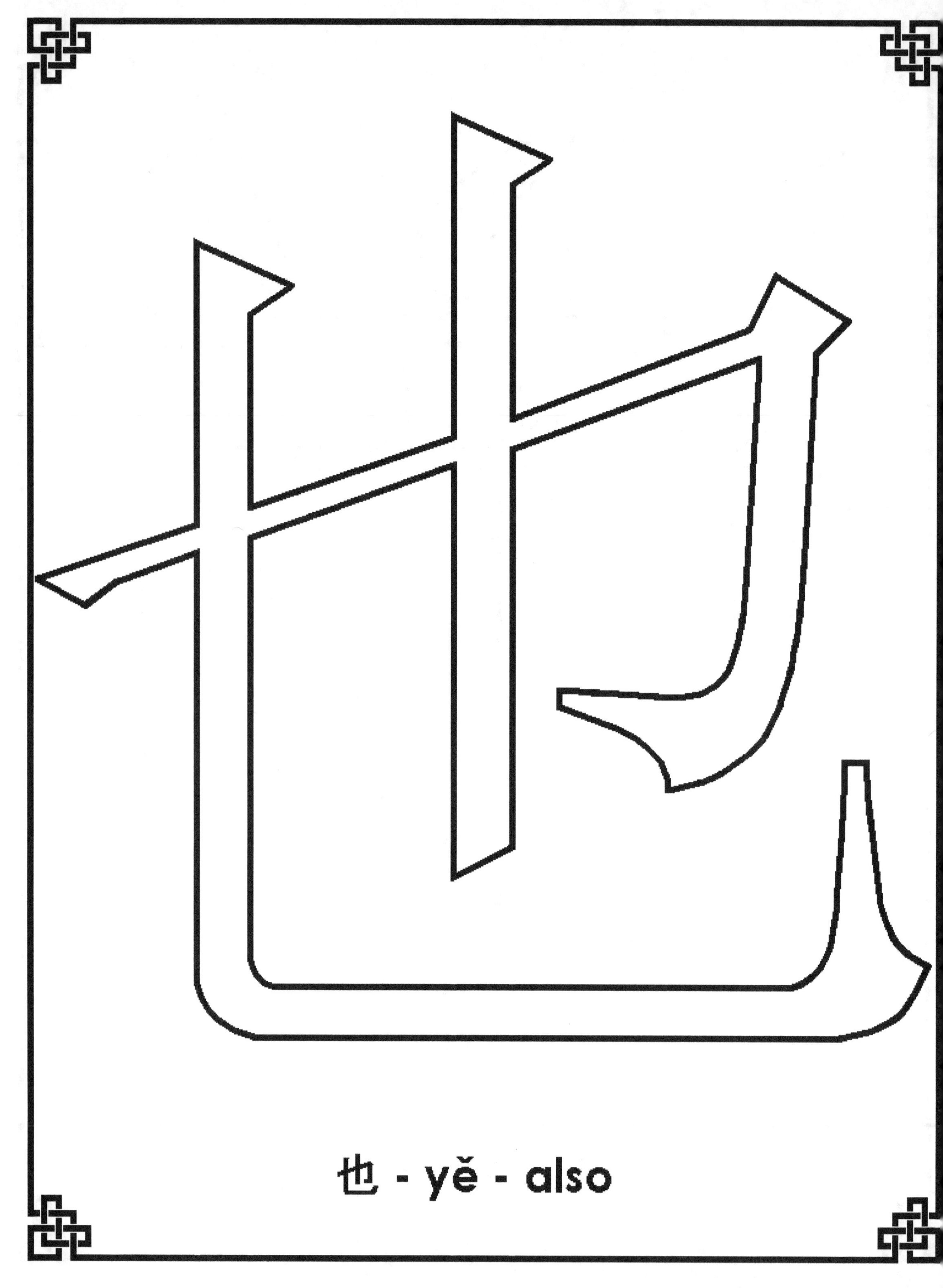

也 - yě - also

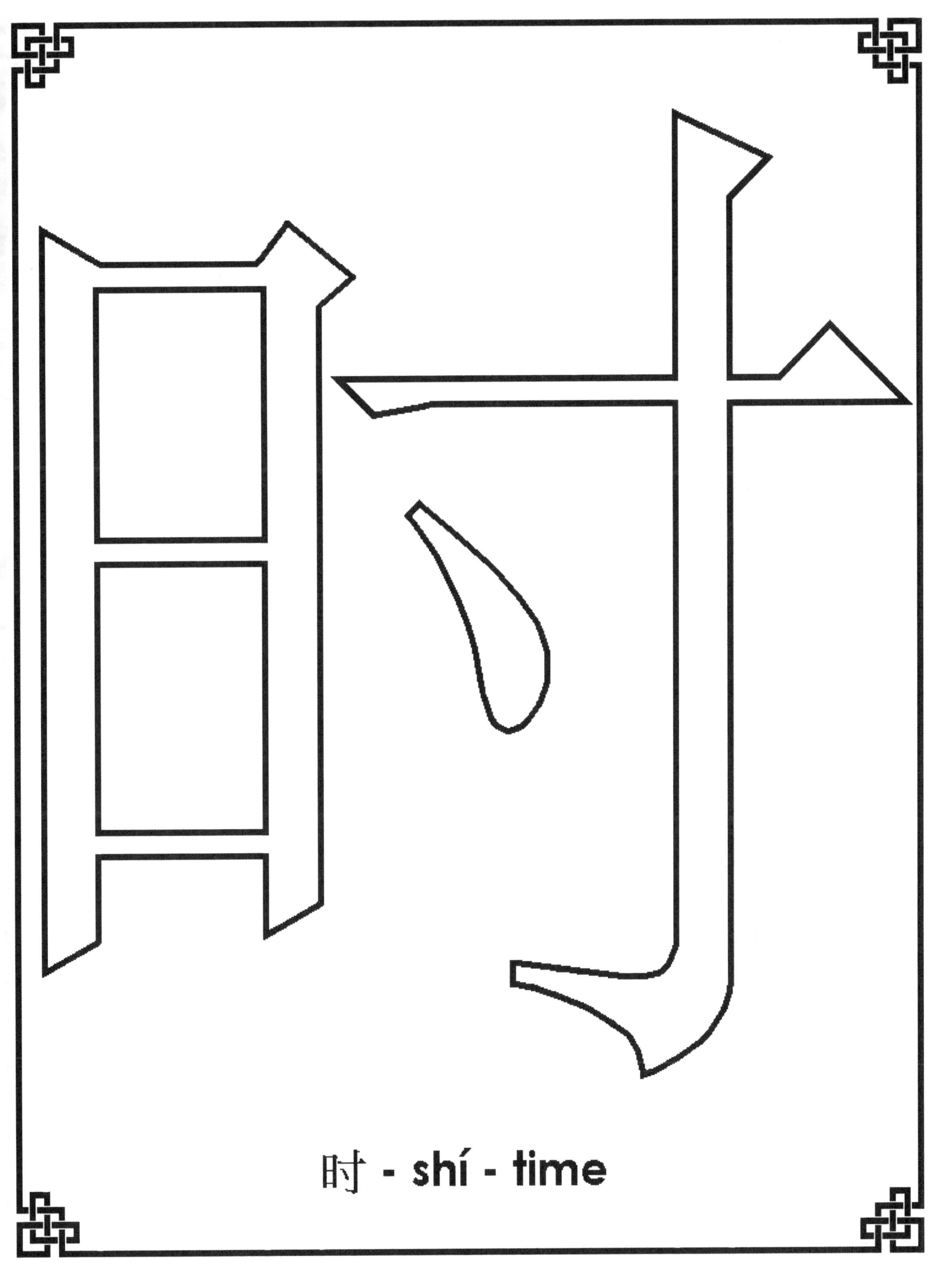

时 - shí - time

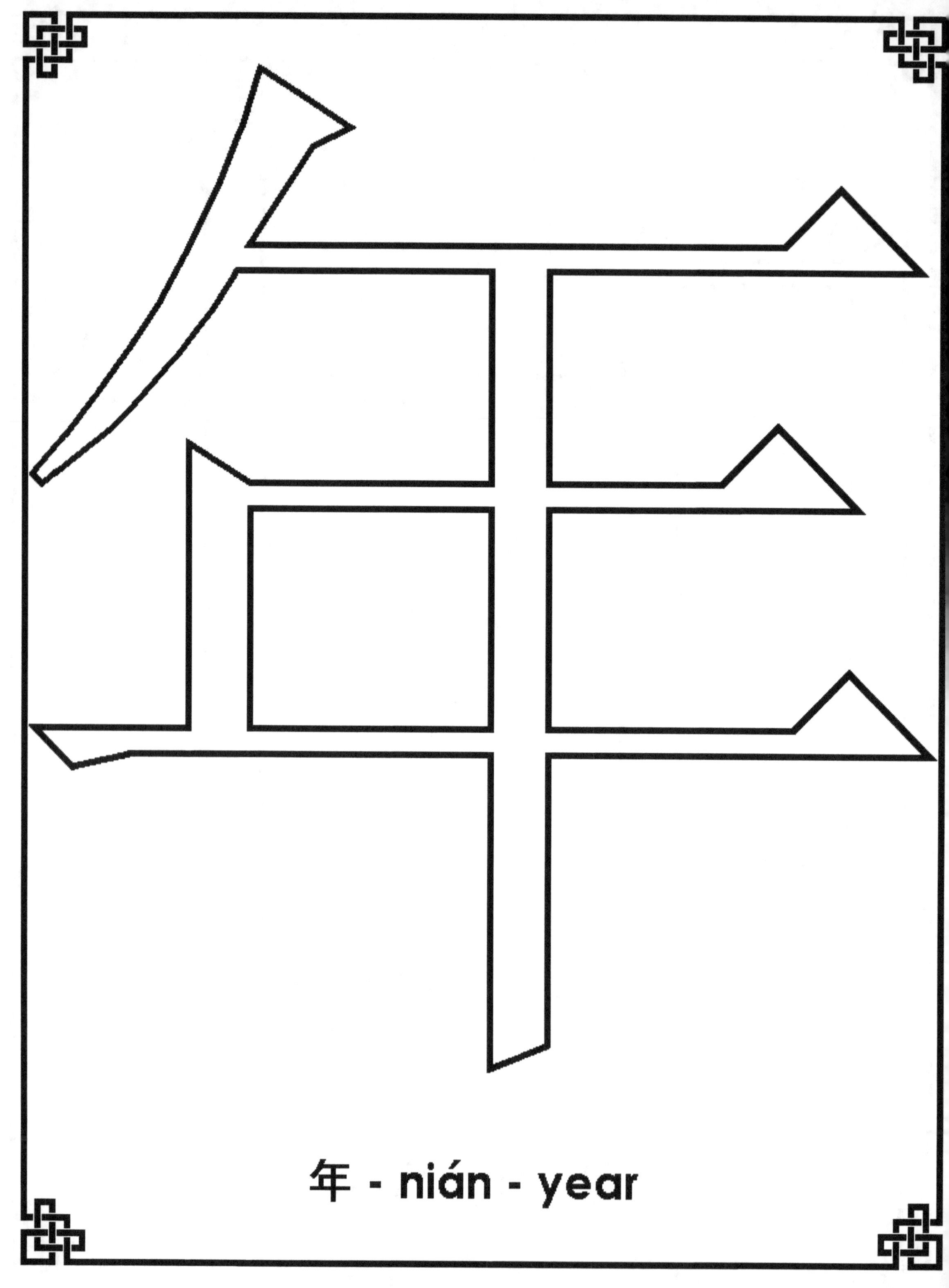

年 - nián - year

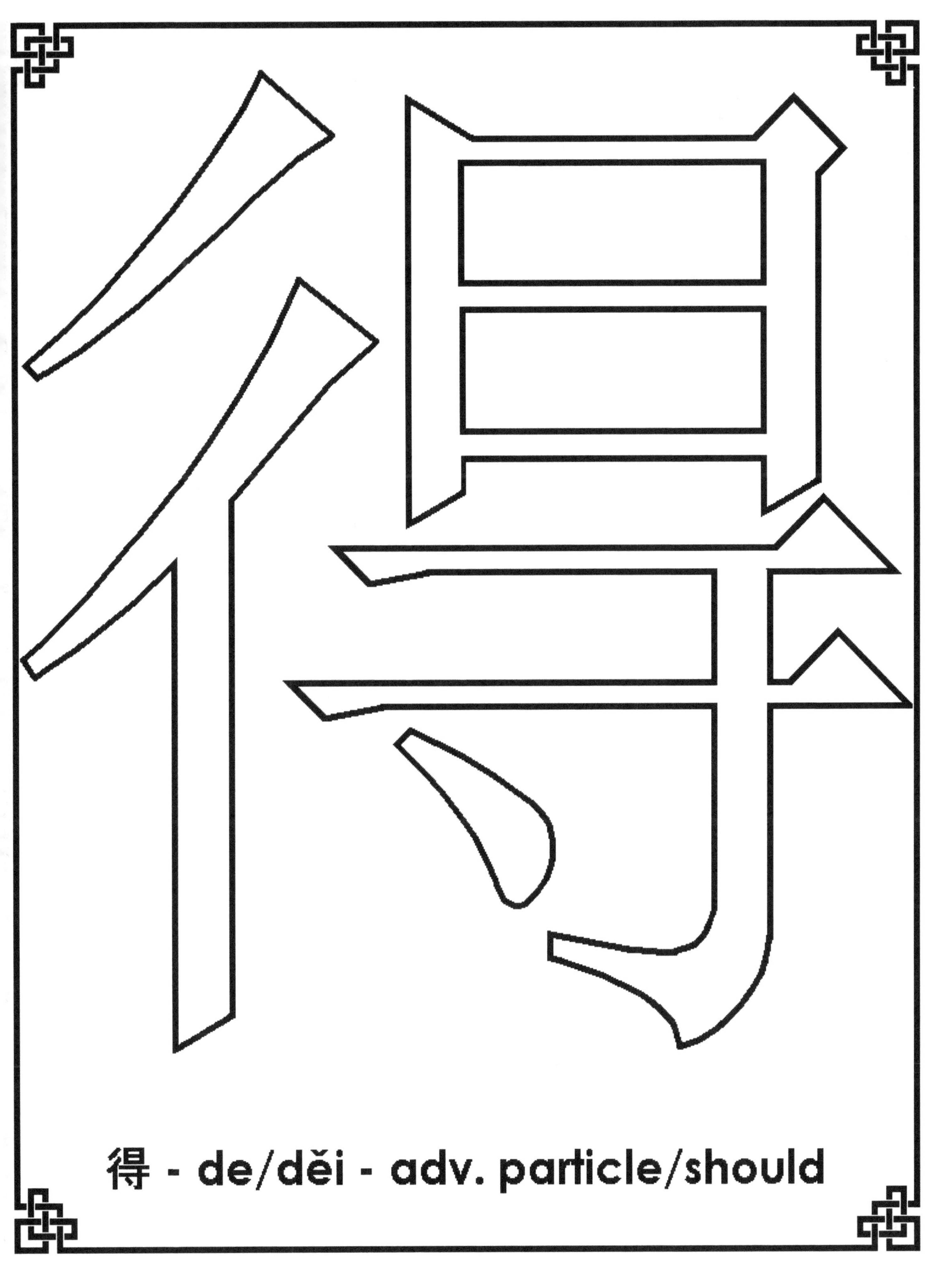

得 - de/děi - adv. particle/should

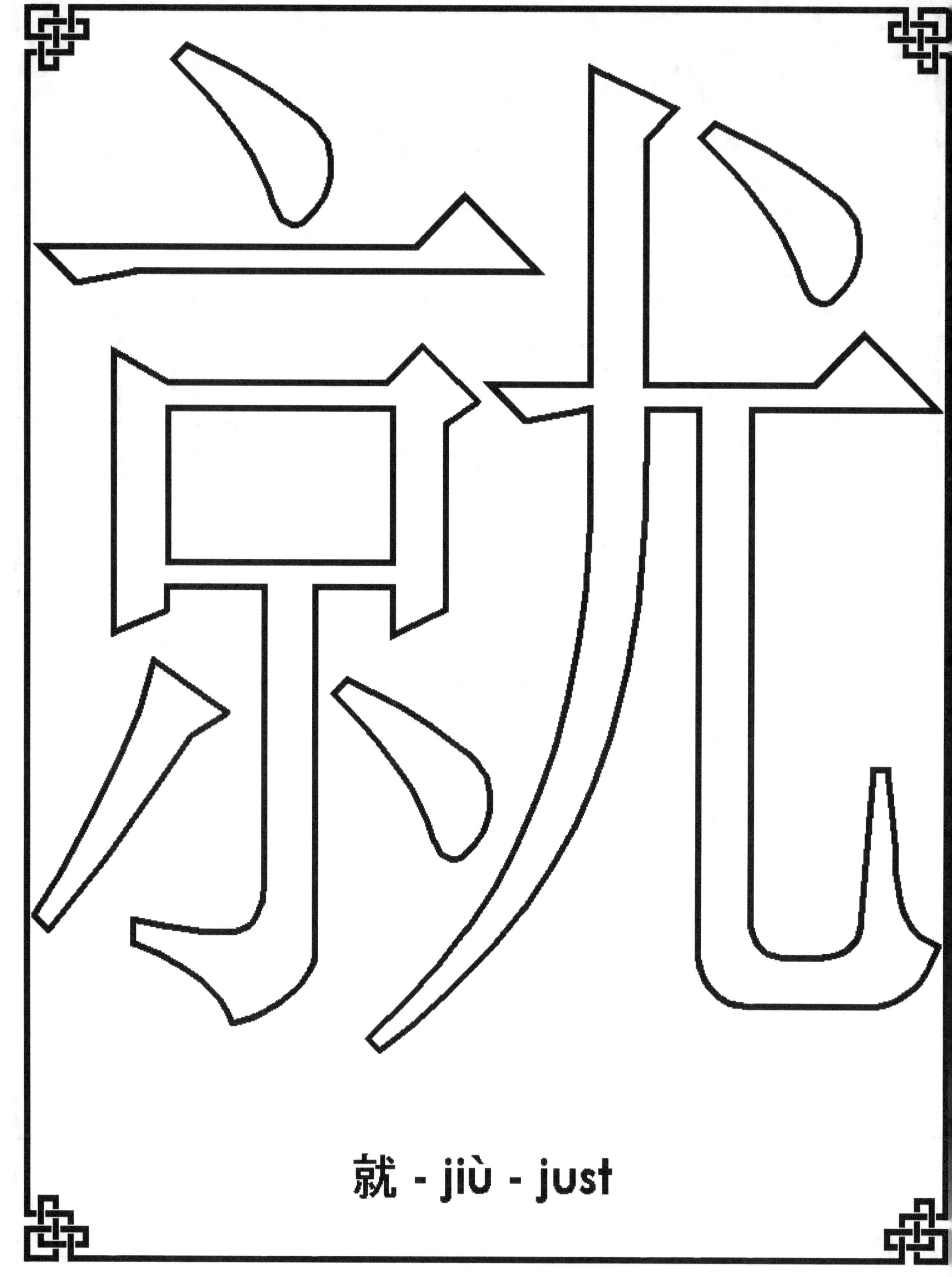

就 - jiù - just

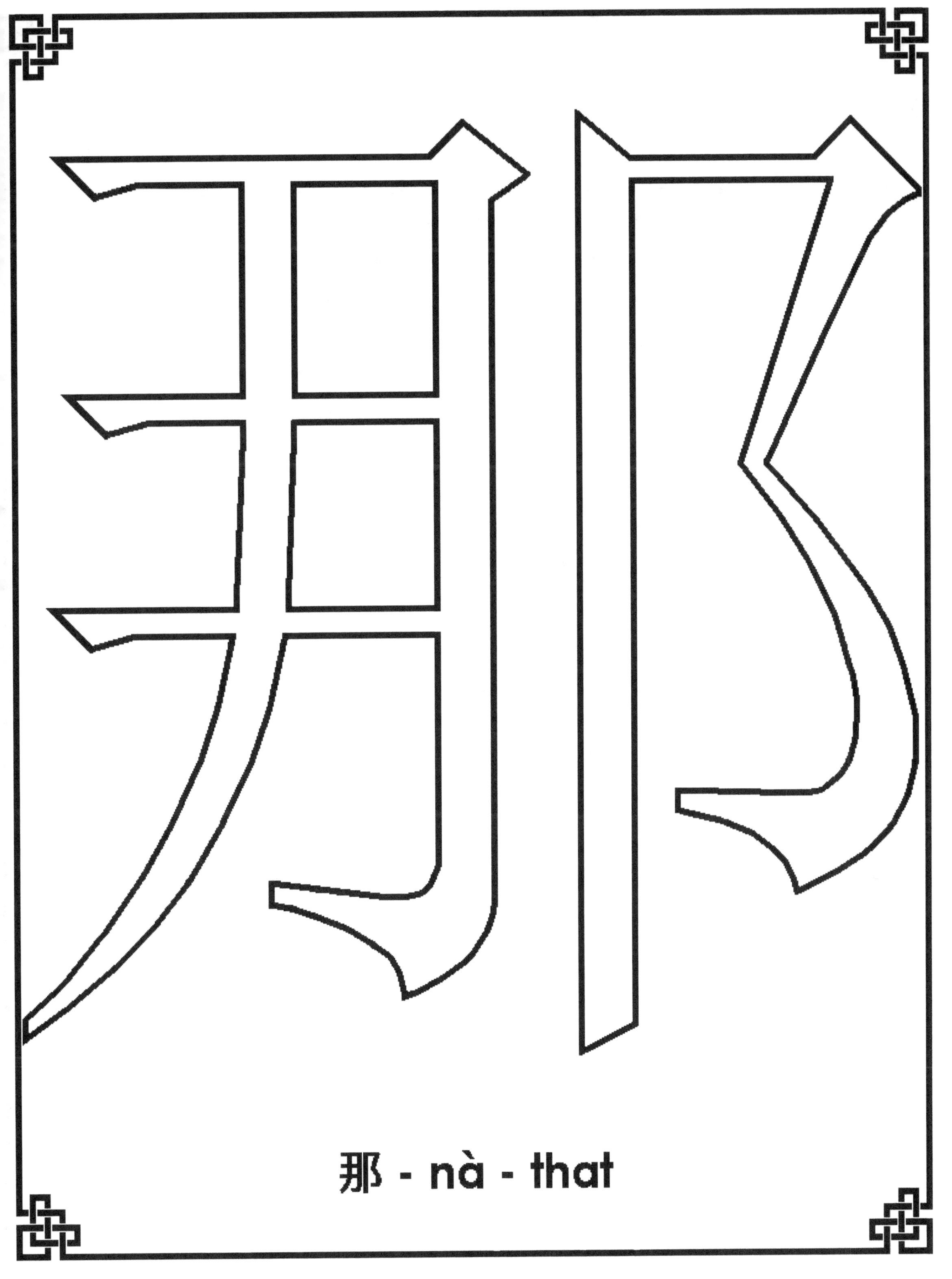

那 - nà - that

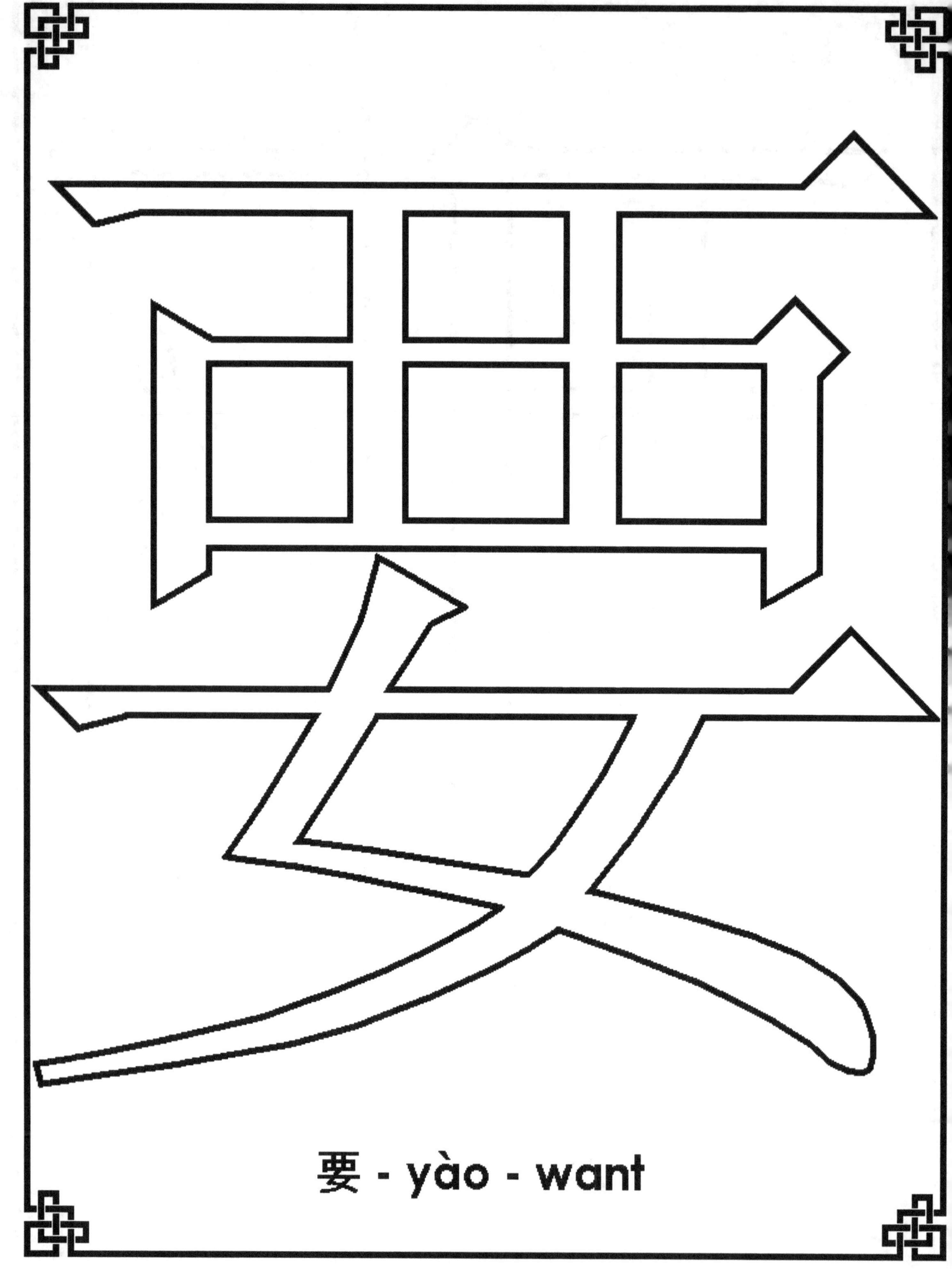

要 - yào - want

下 - xià - down

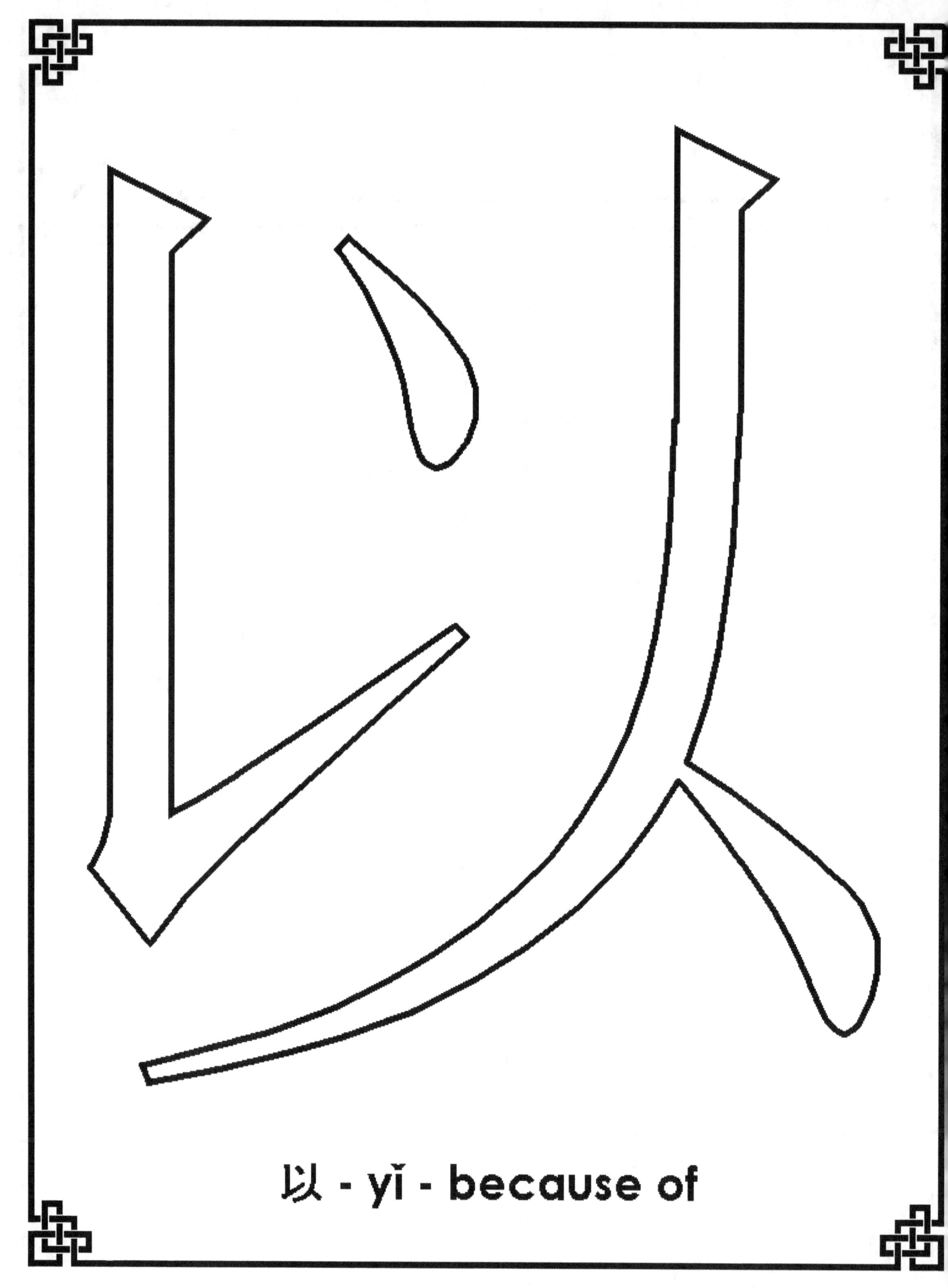

以 - yǐ - because of

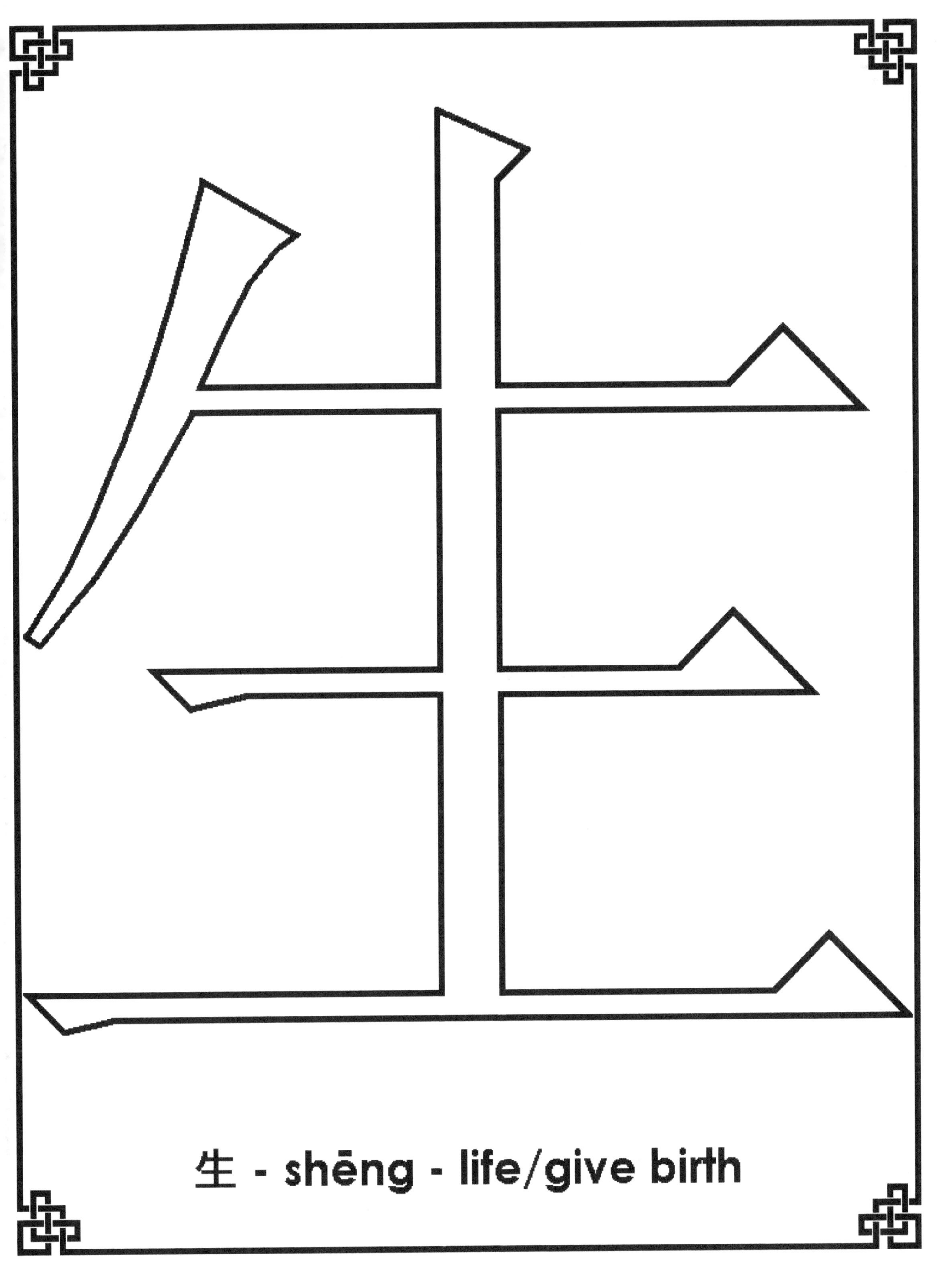

生 - shēng - life/give birth

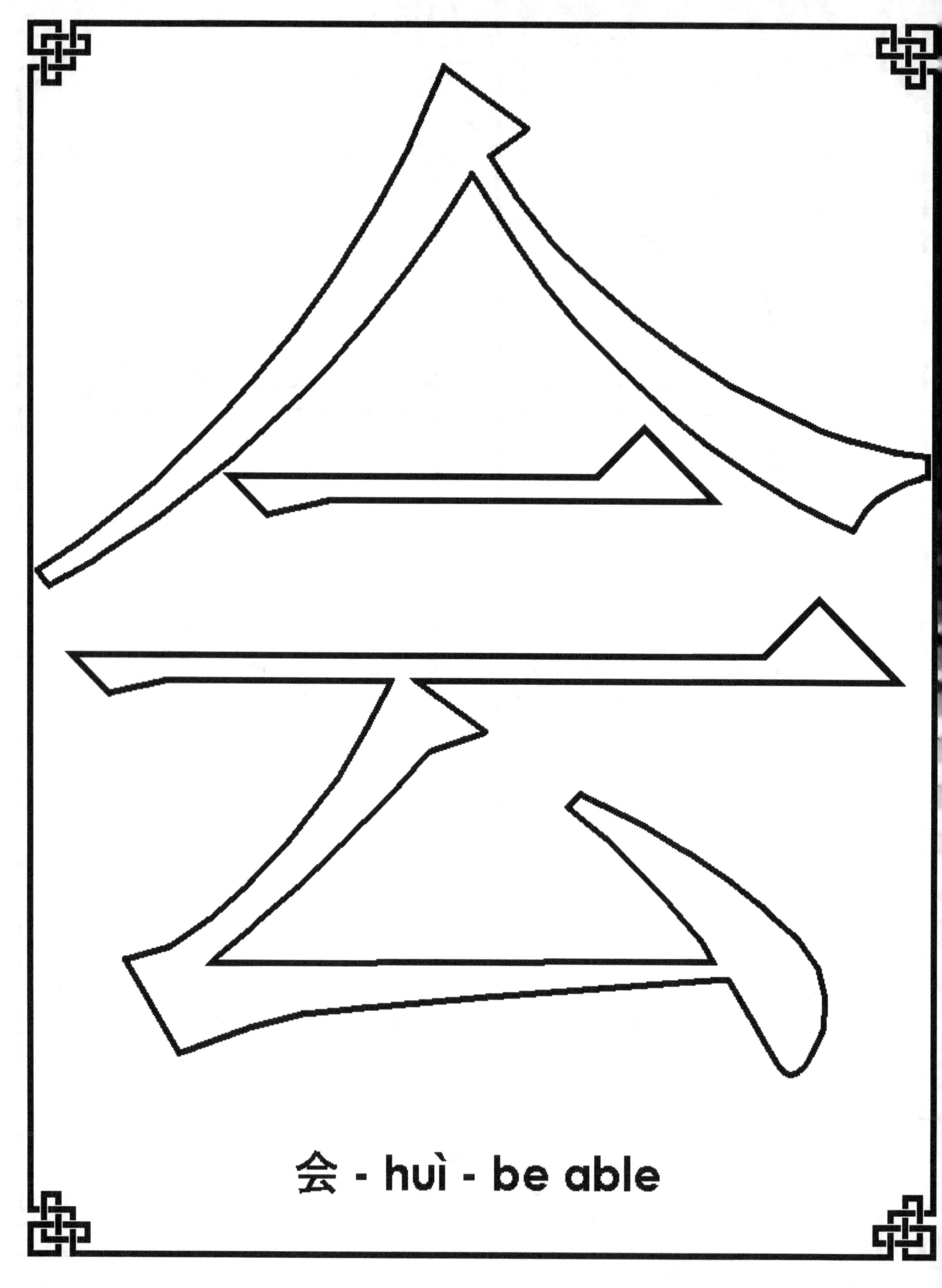

会 - huì - be able

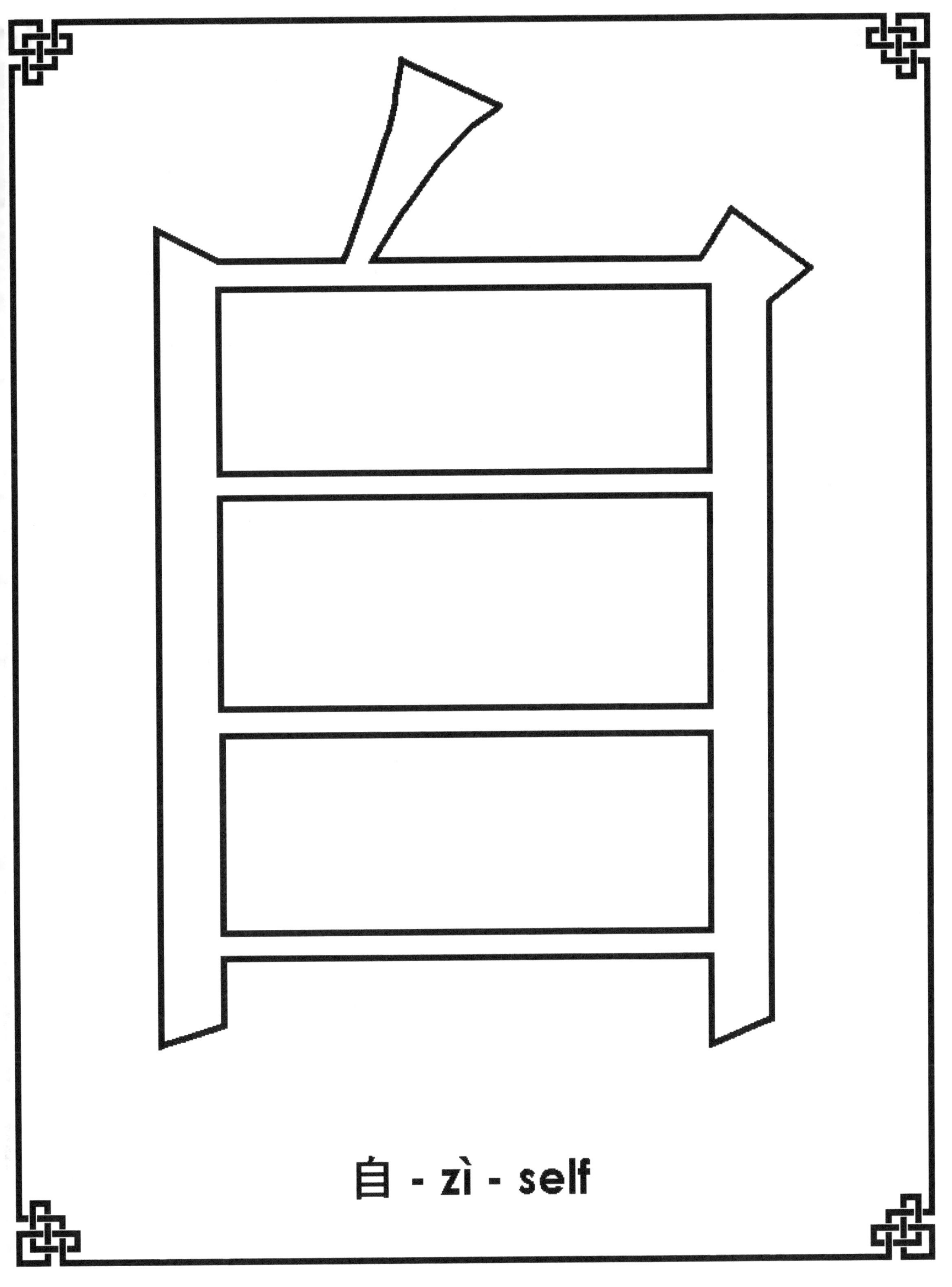

自 - zì - self

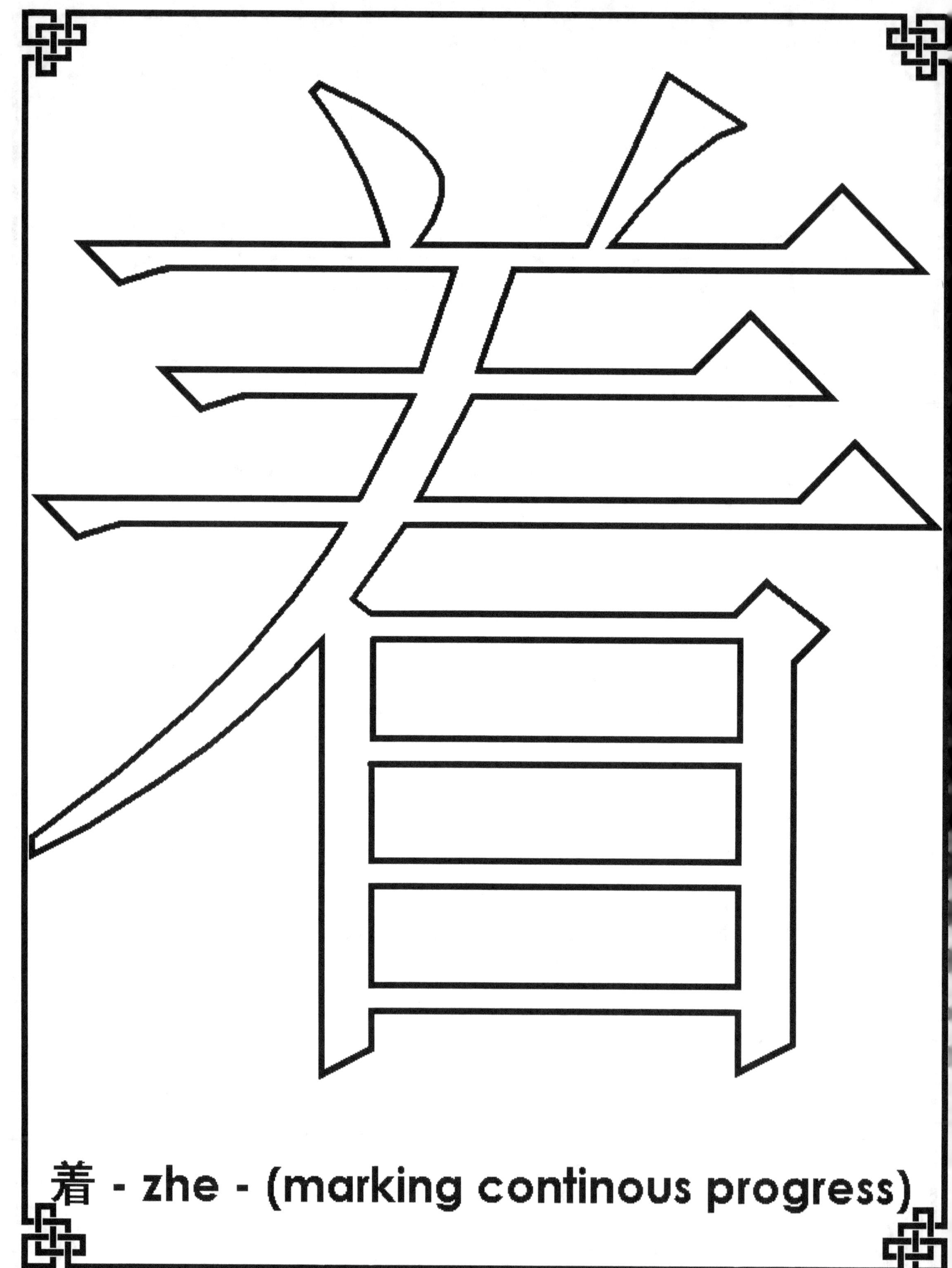

着 - zhe - (marking continous progress)

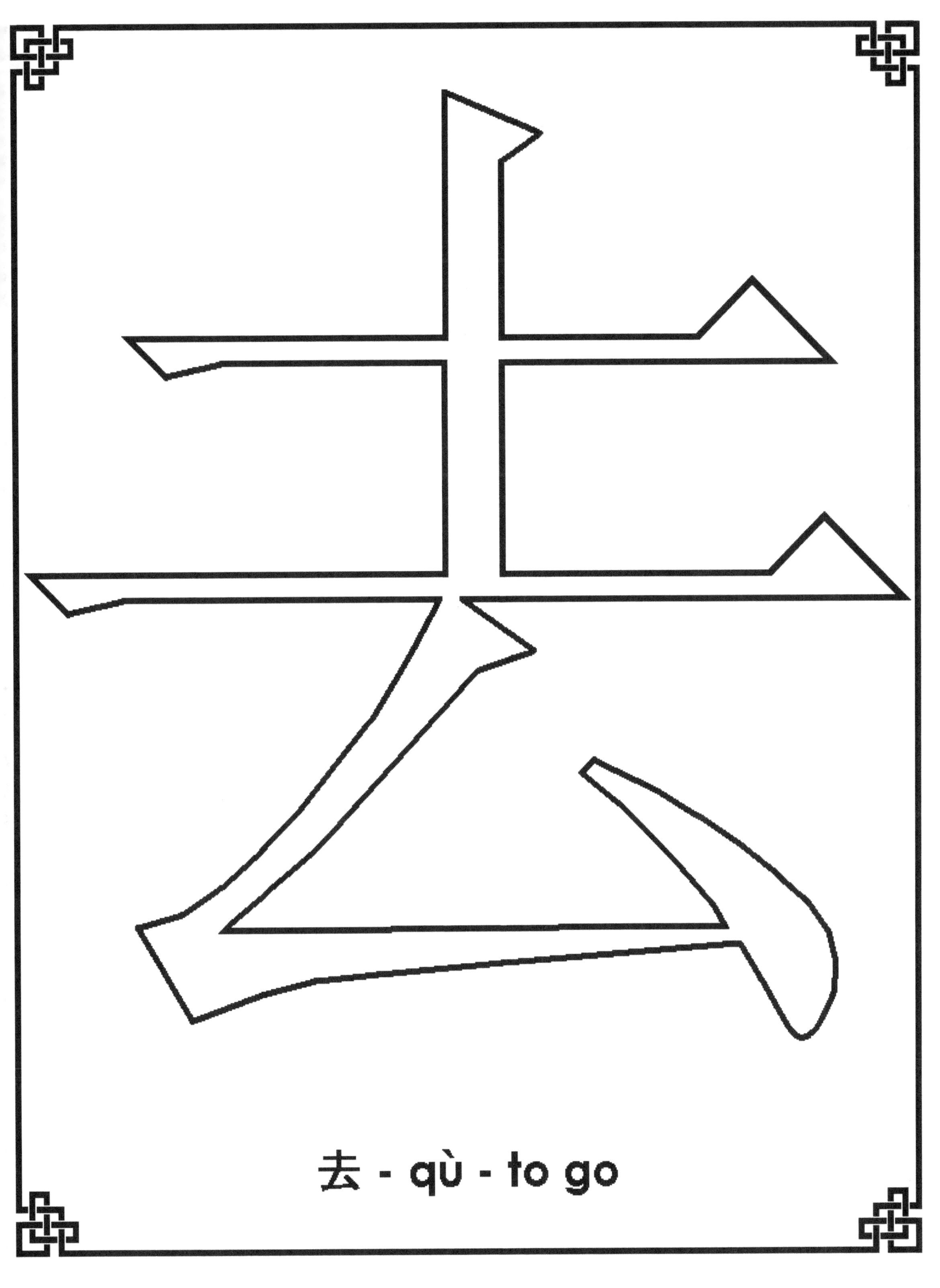

去 - qù - to go

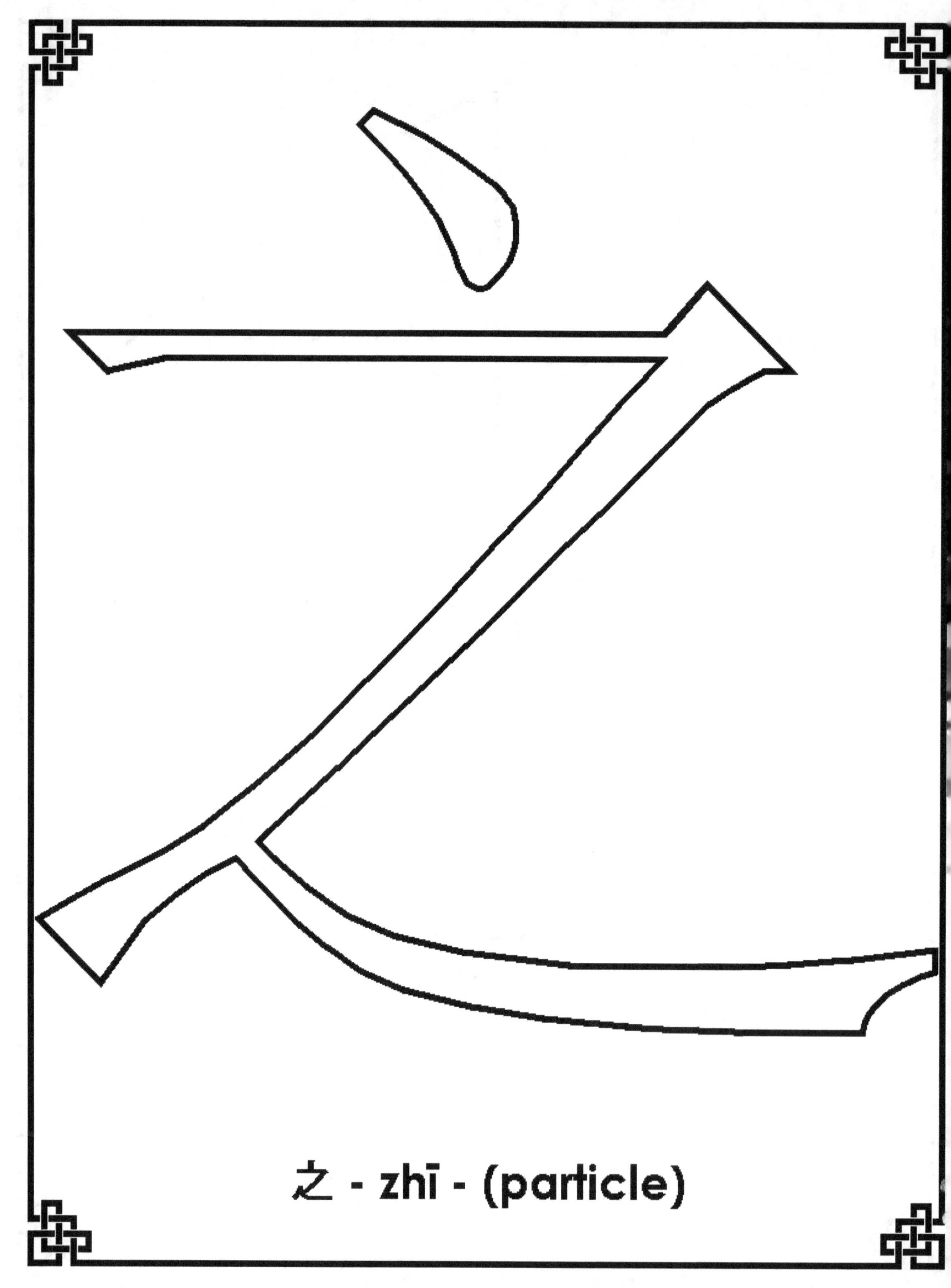

之 - zhī - (particle)

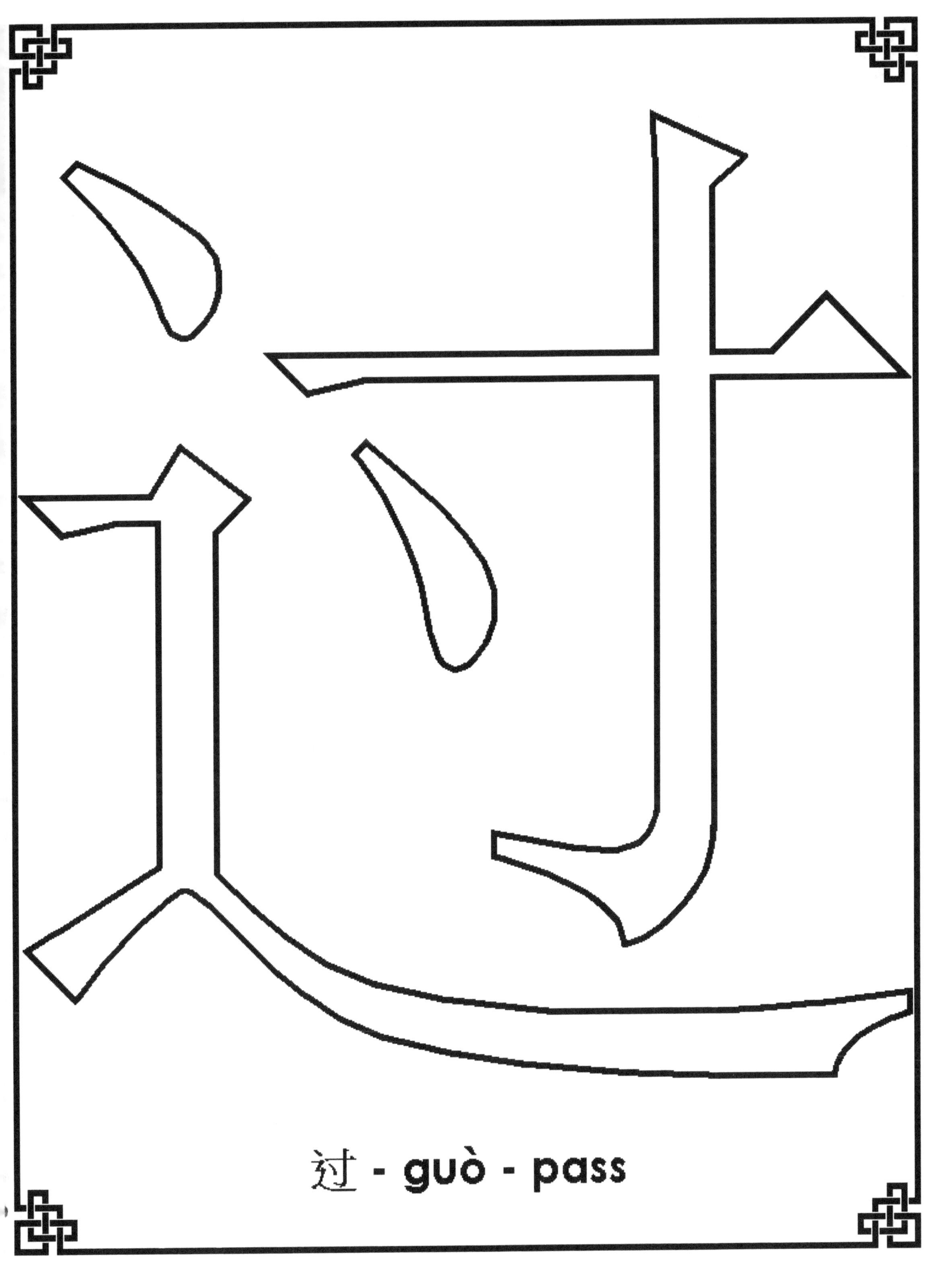

过 - guò - pass

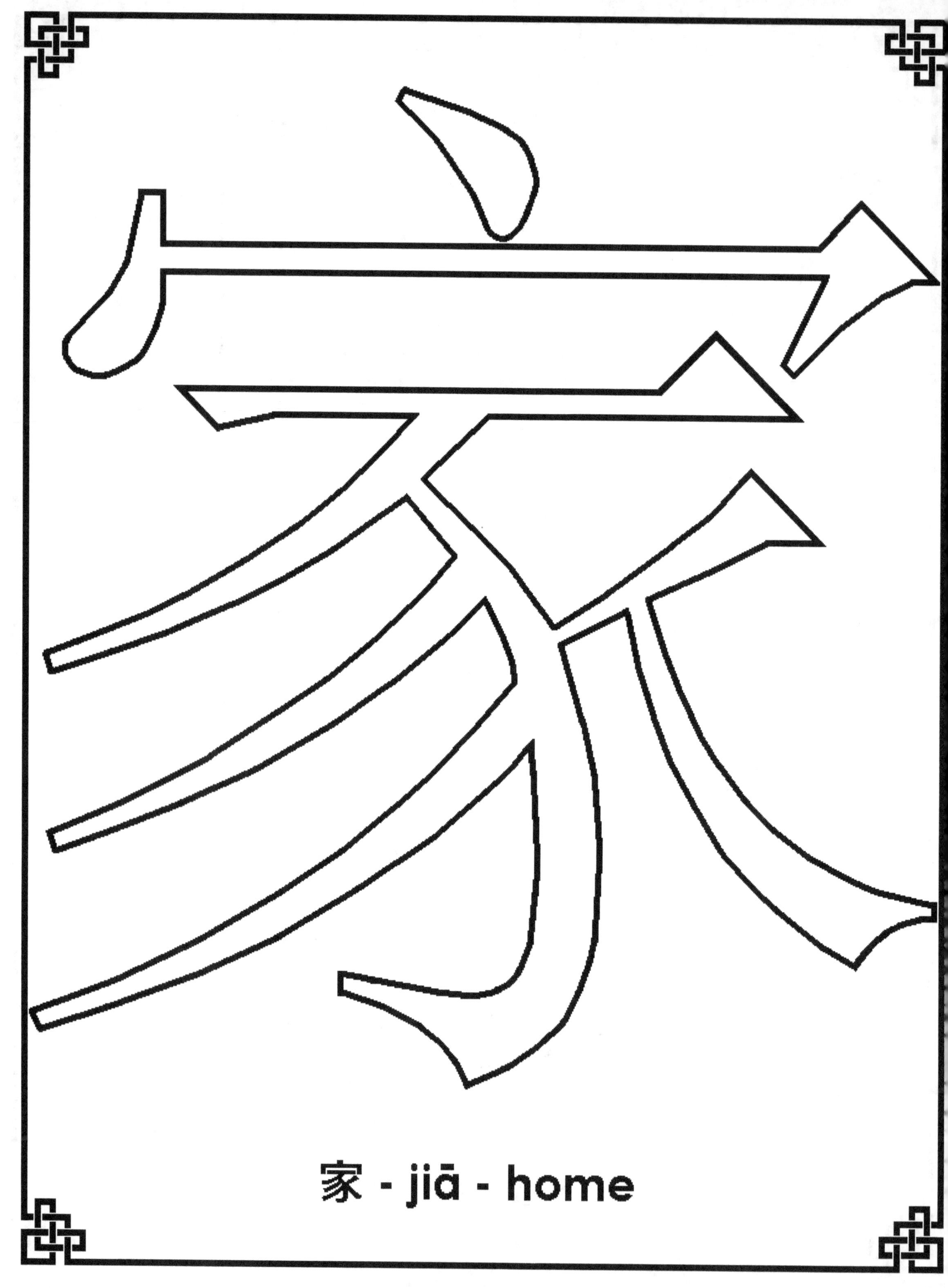

家 - jiā - home

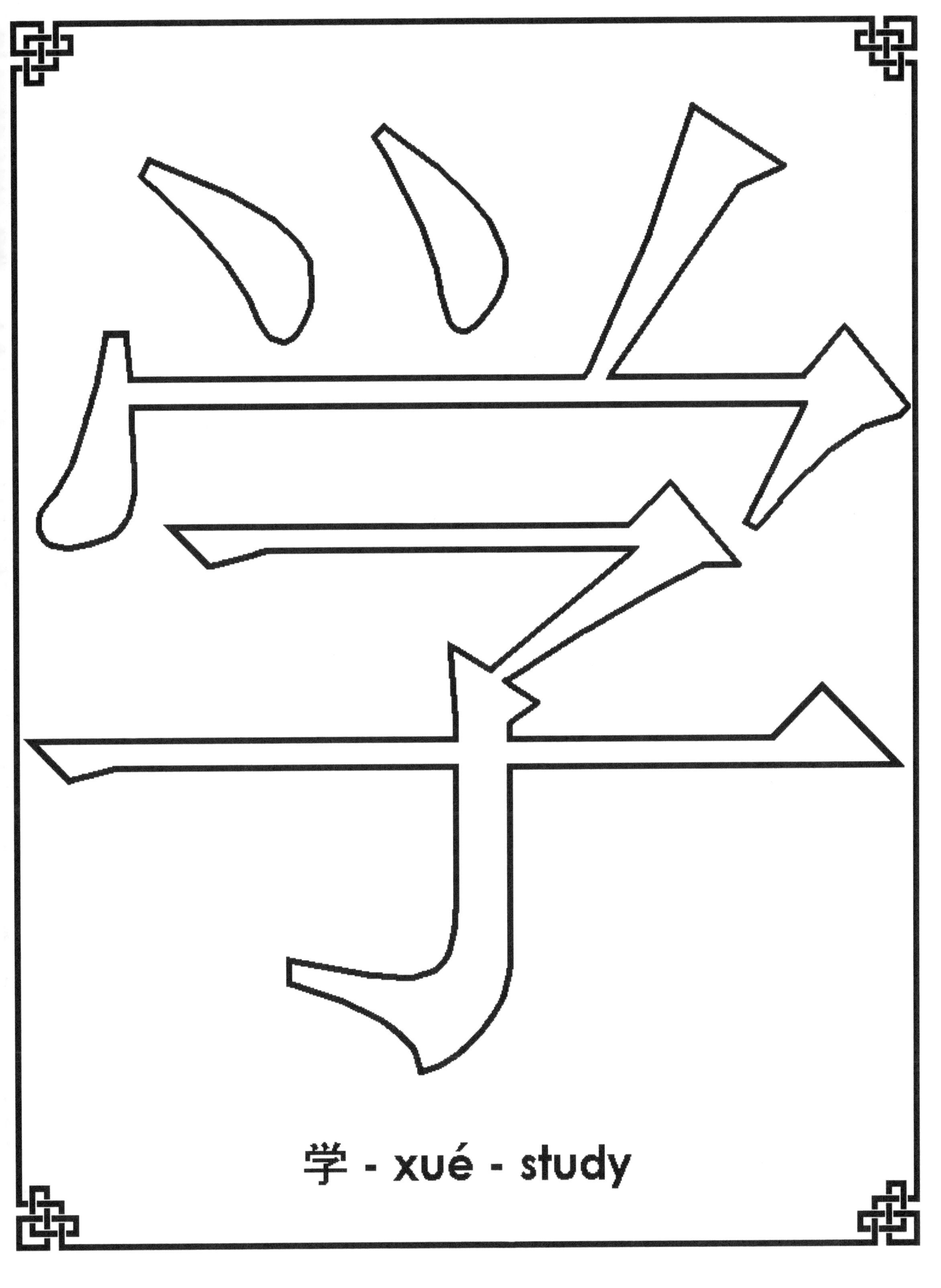

学 - xué - study

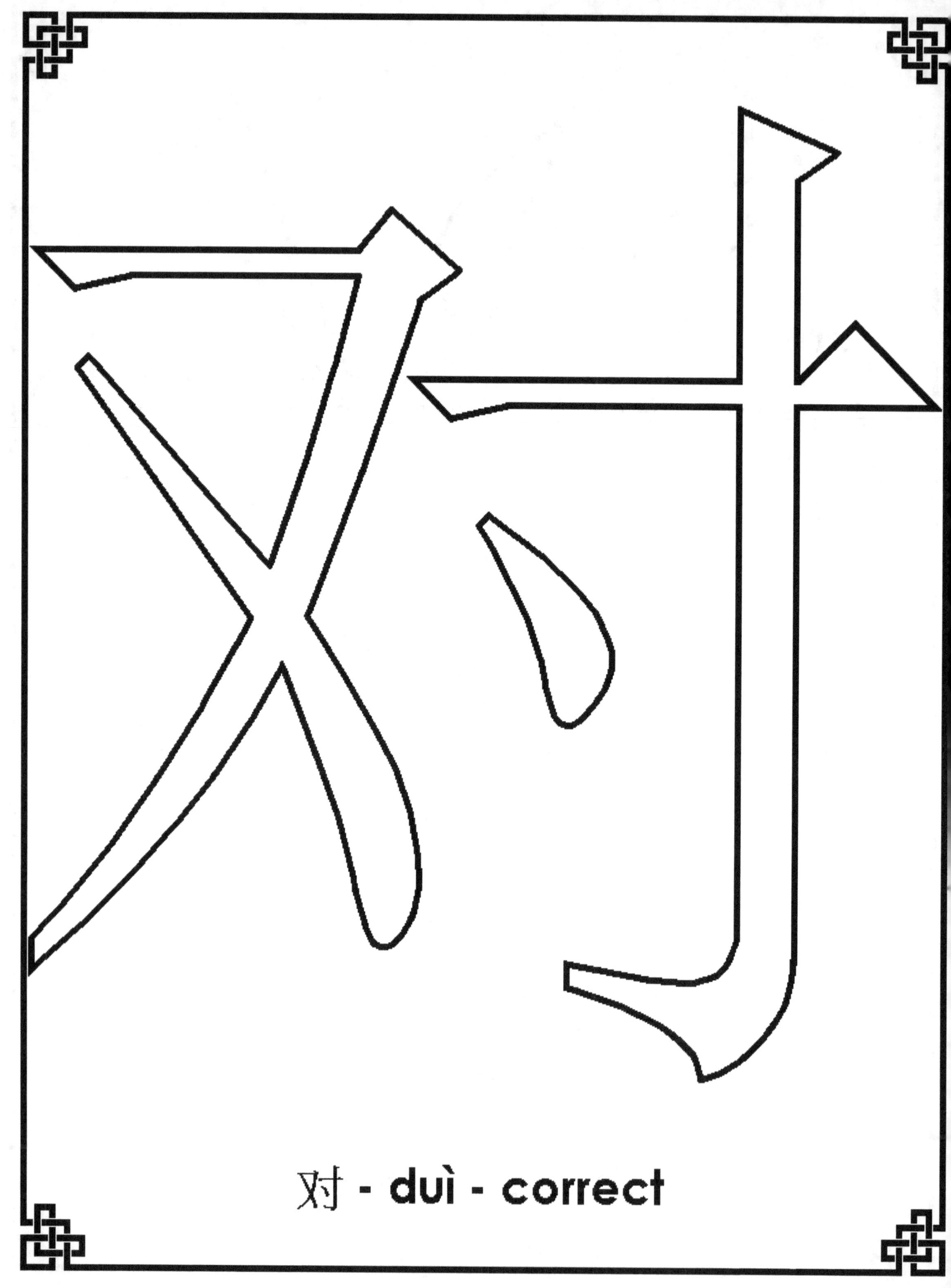

对 - duì - correct

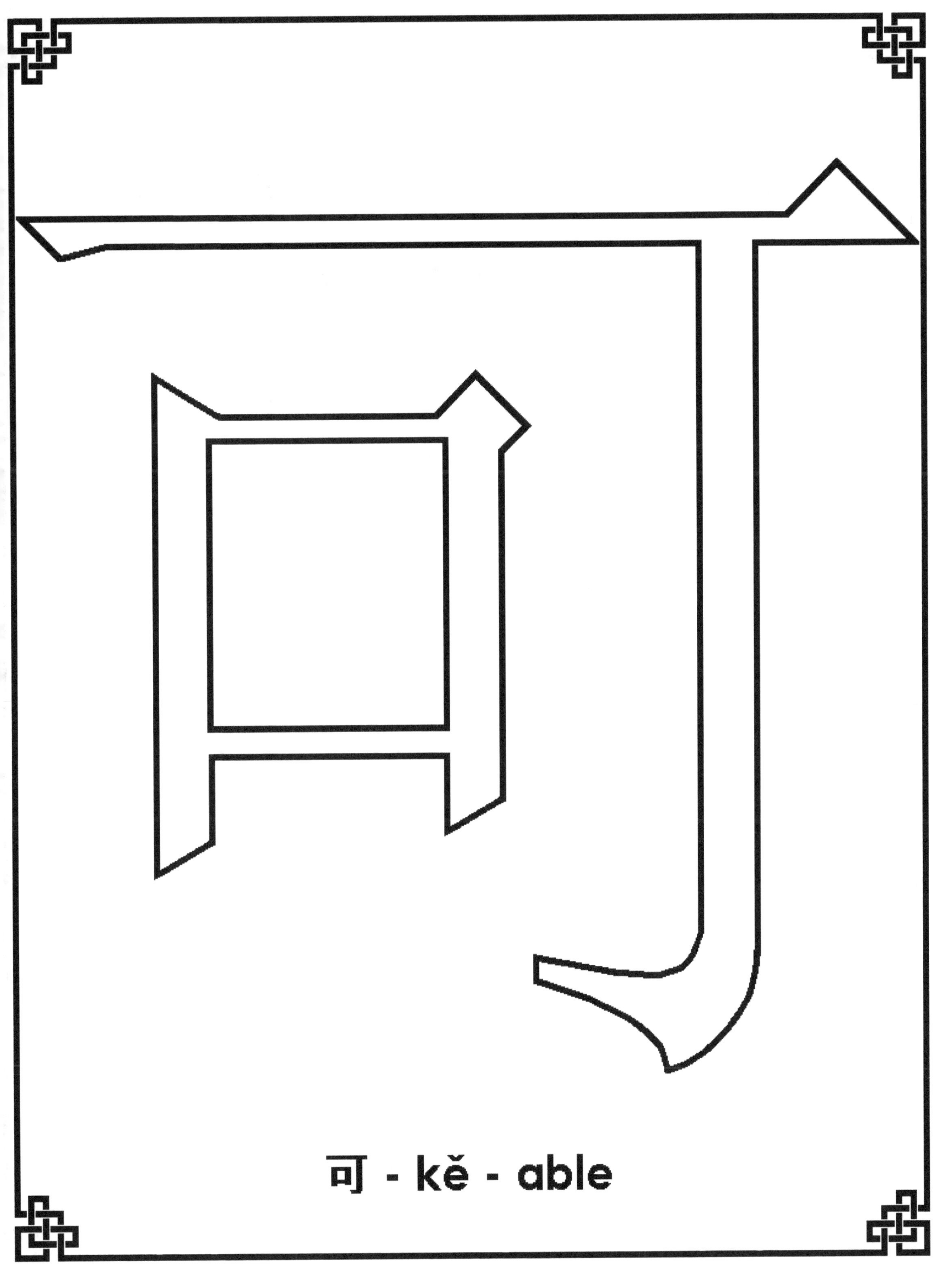

可 - kě - able

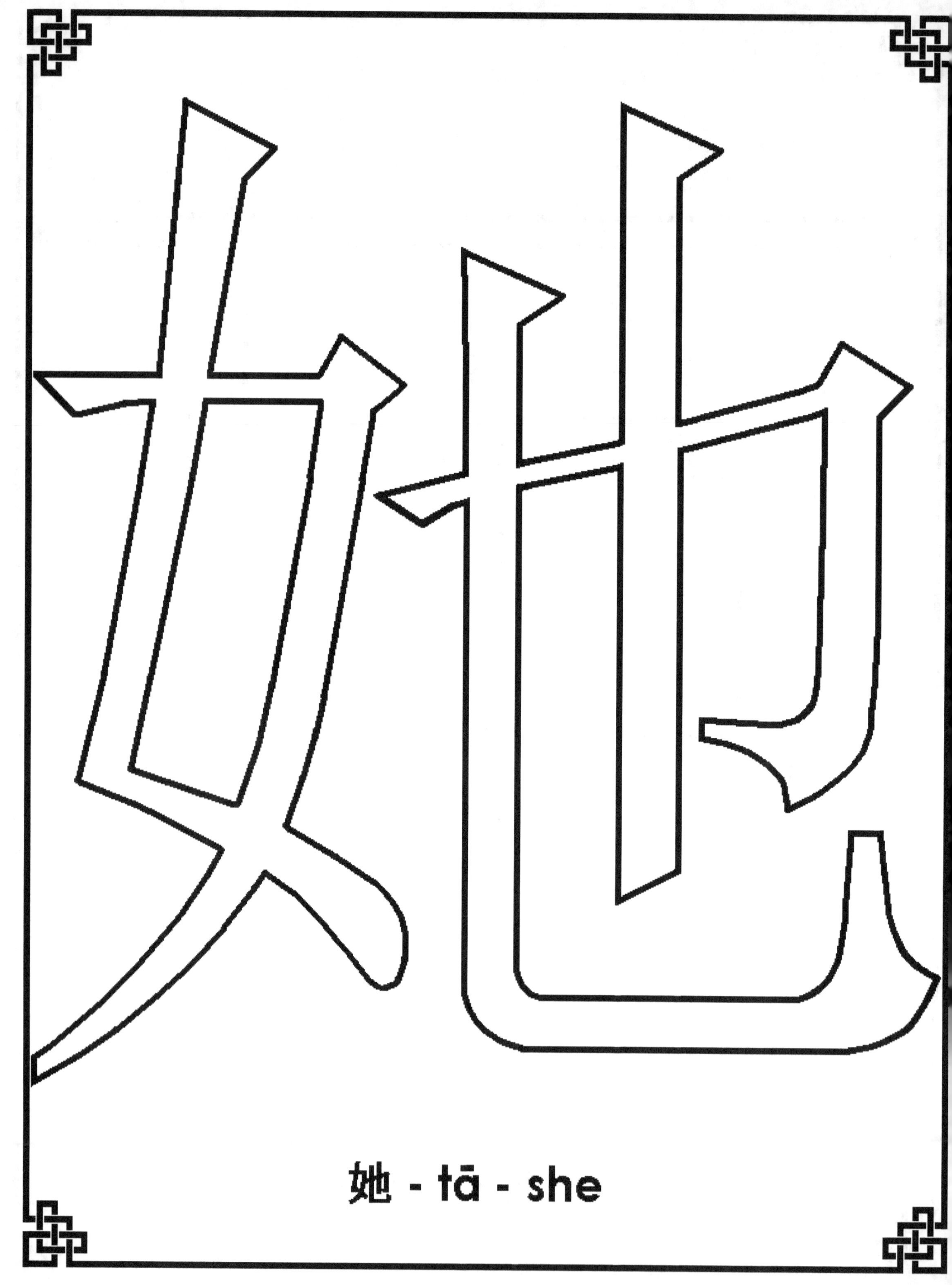

她 - tā - she

里 - lǐ - inside

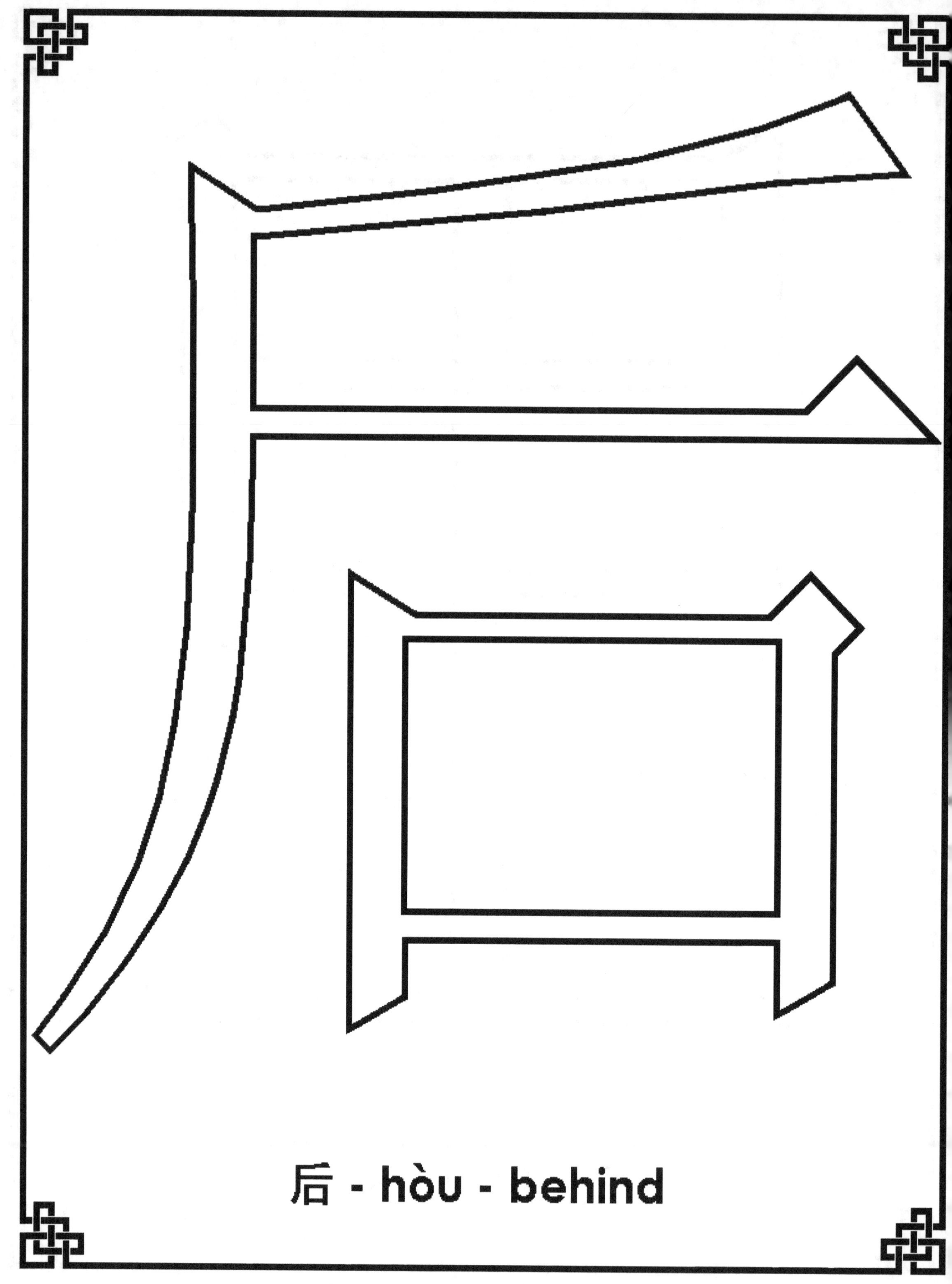

后 - hòu - behind

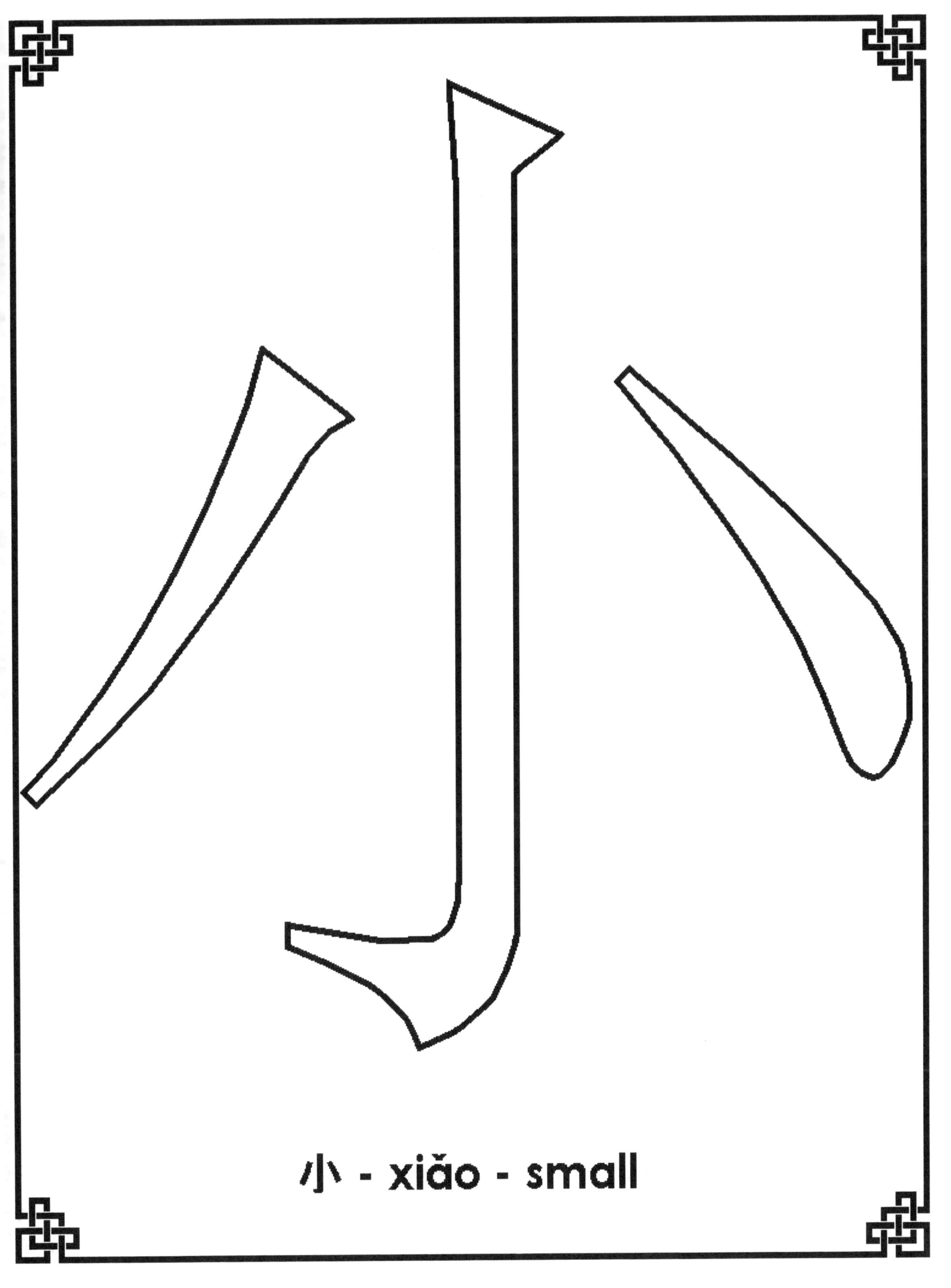

小 - xiǎo - small

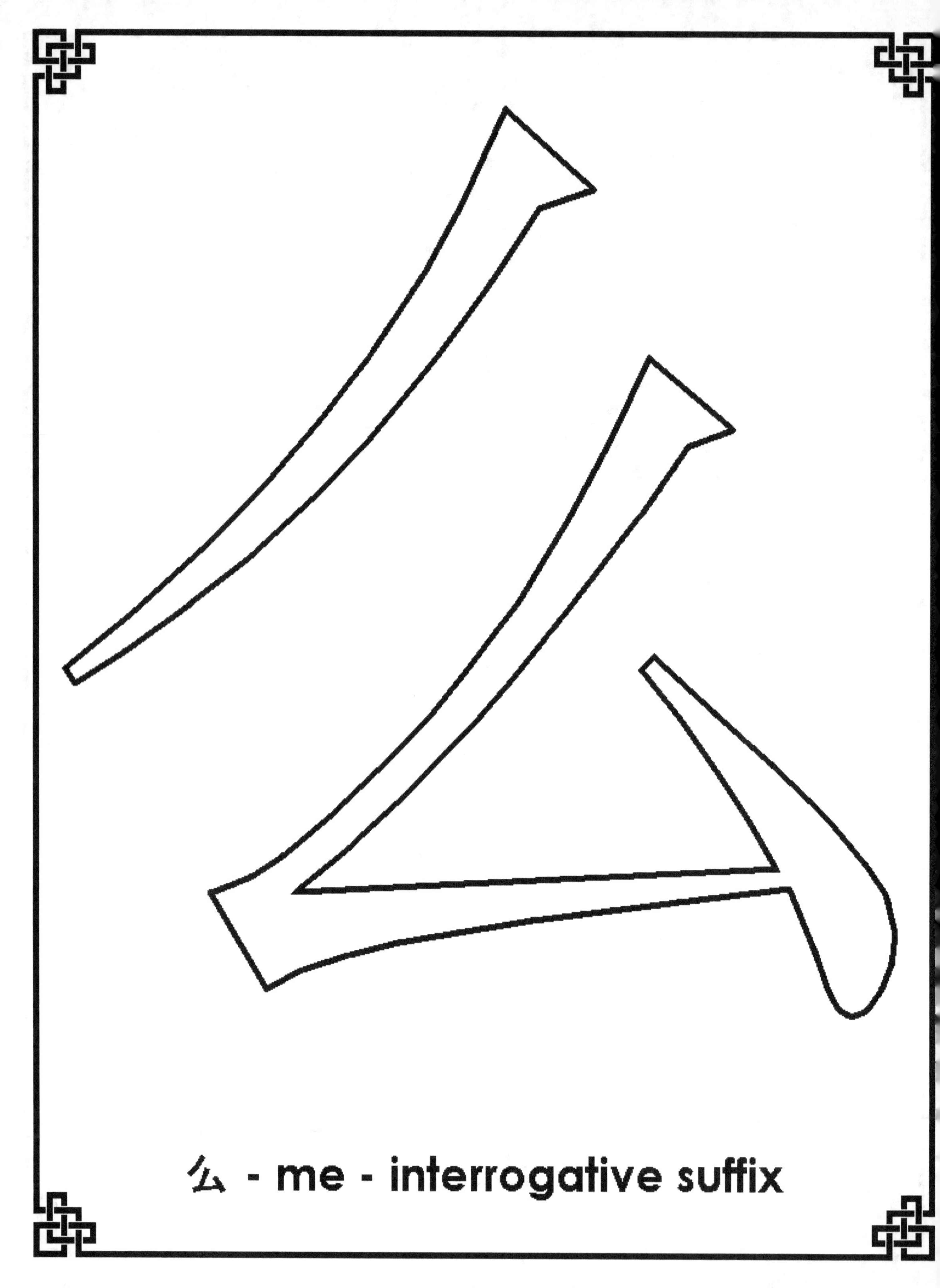

么 - me - interrogative suffix

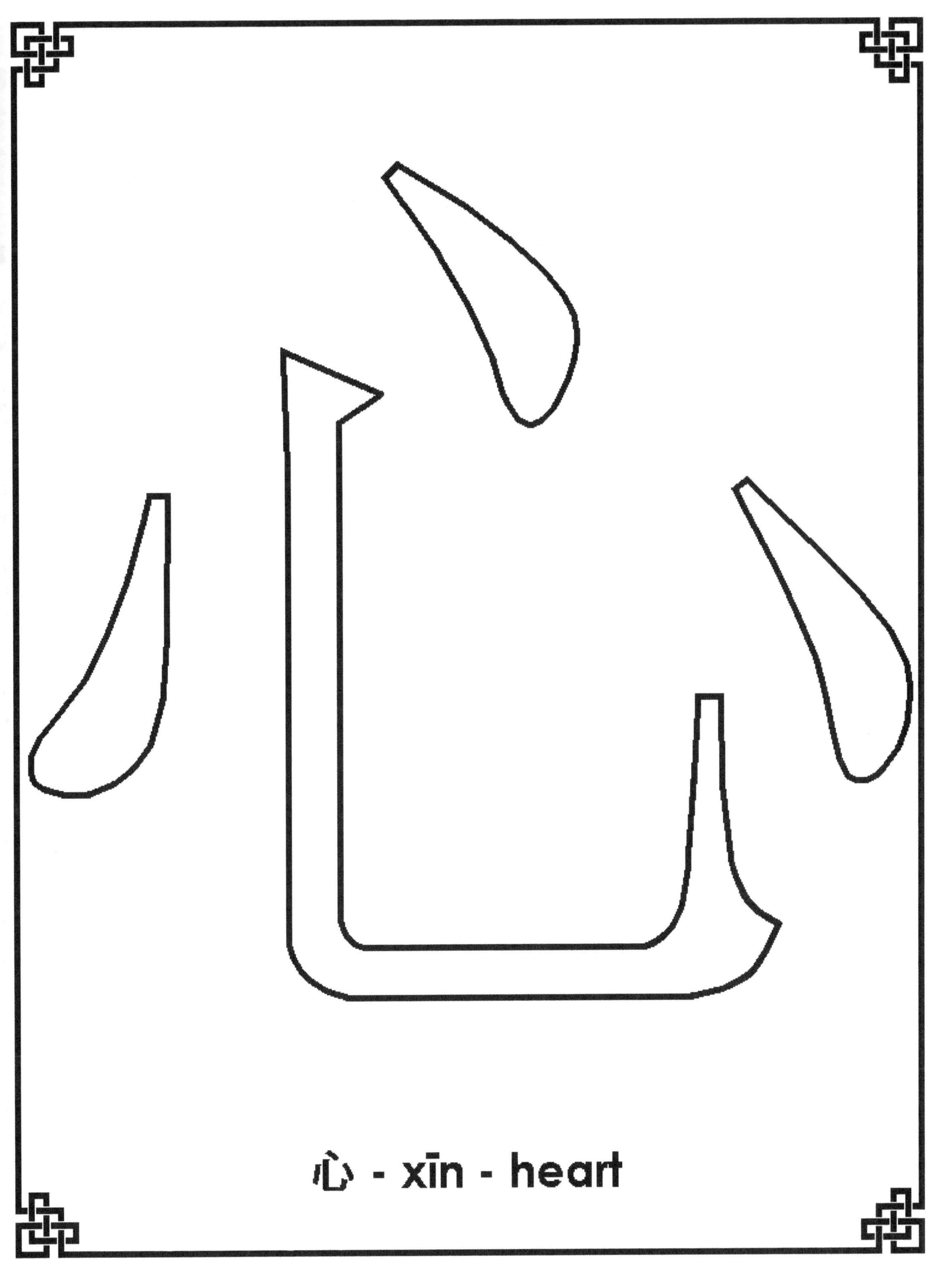

心 - xīn - heart

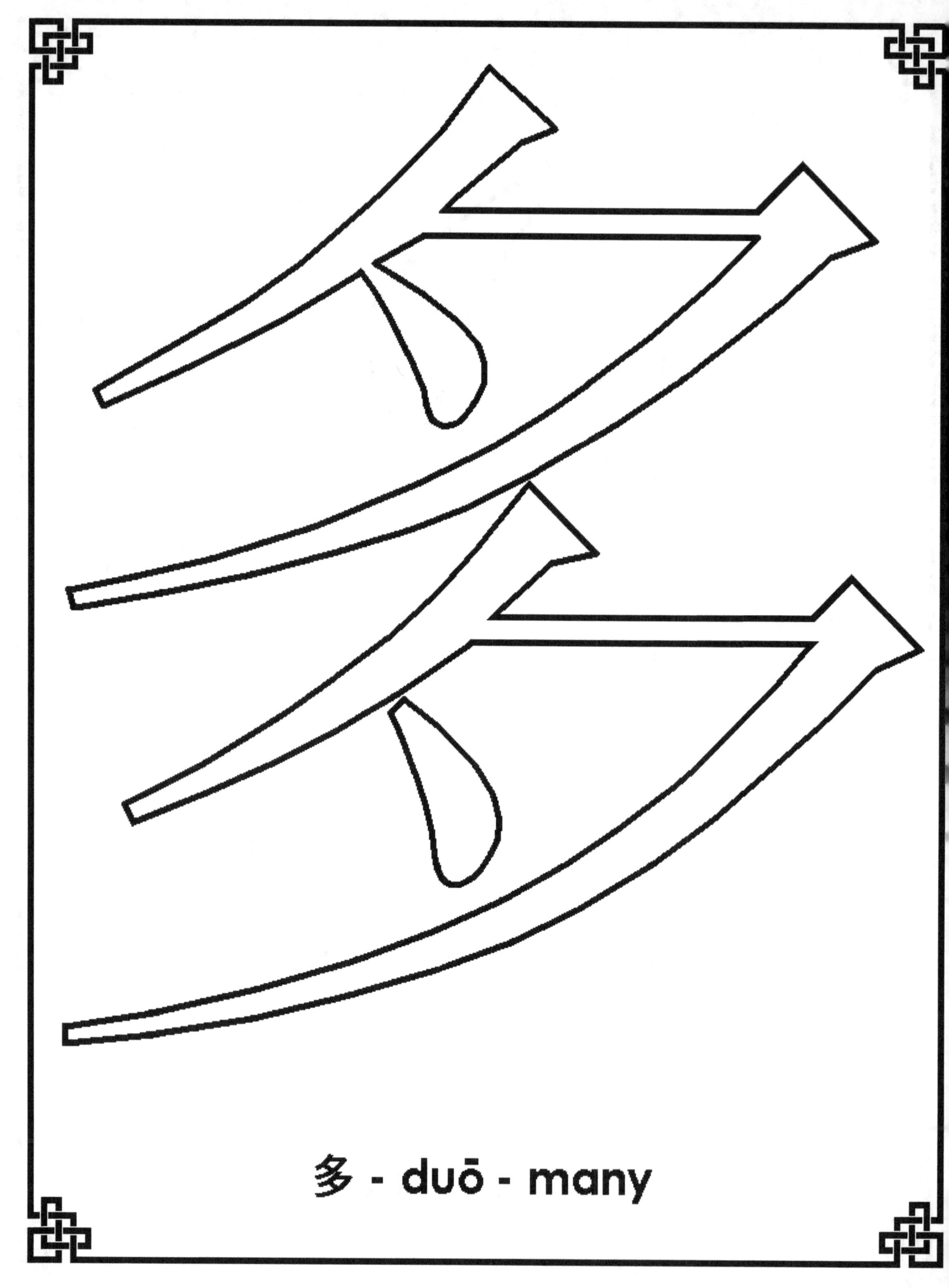

多 - duō - many

天 - tiān - sky

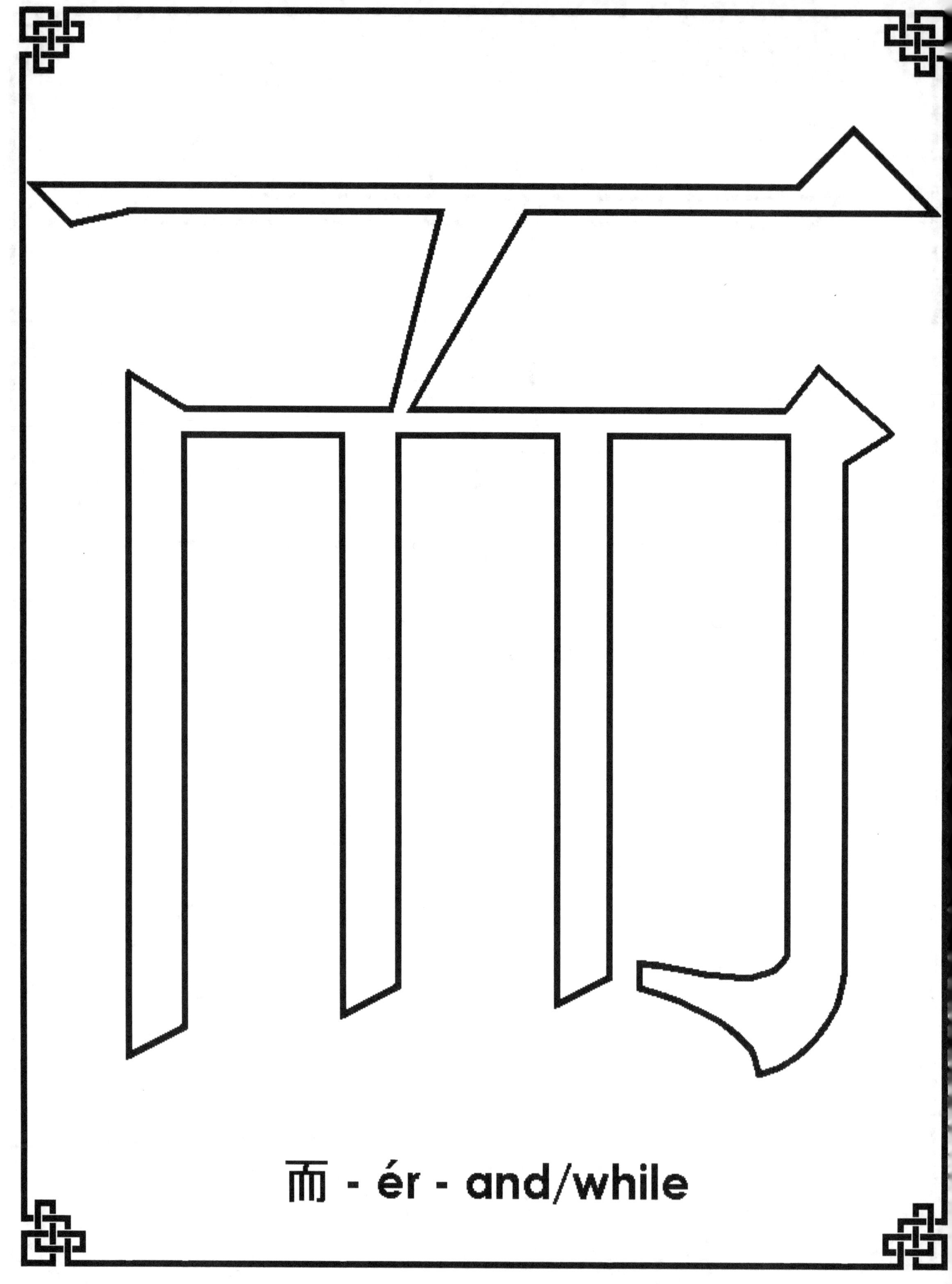

而 - ér - and/while

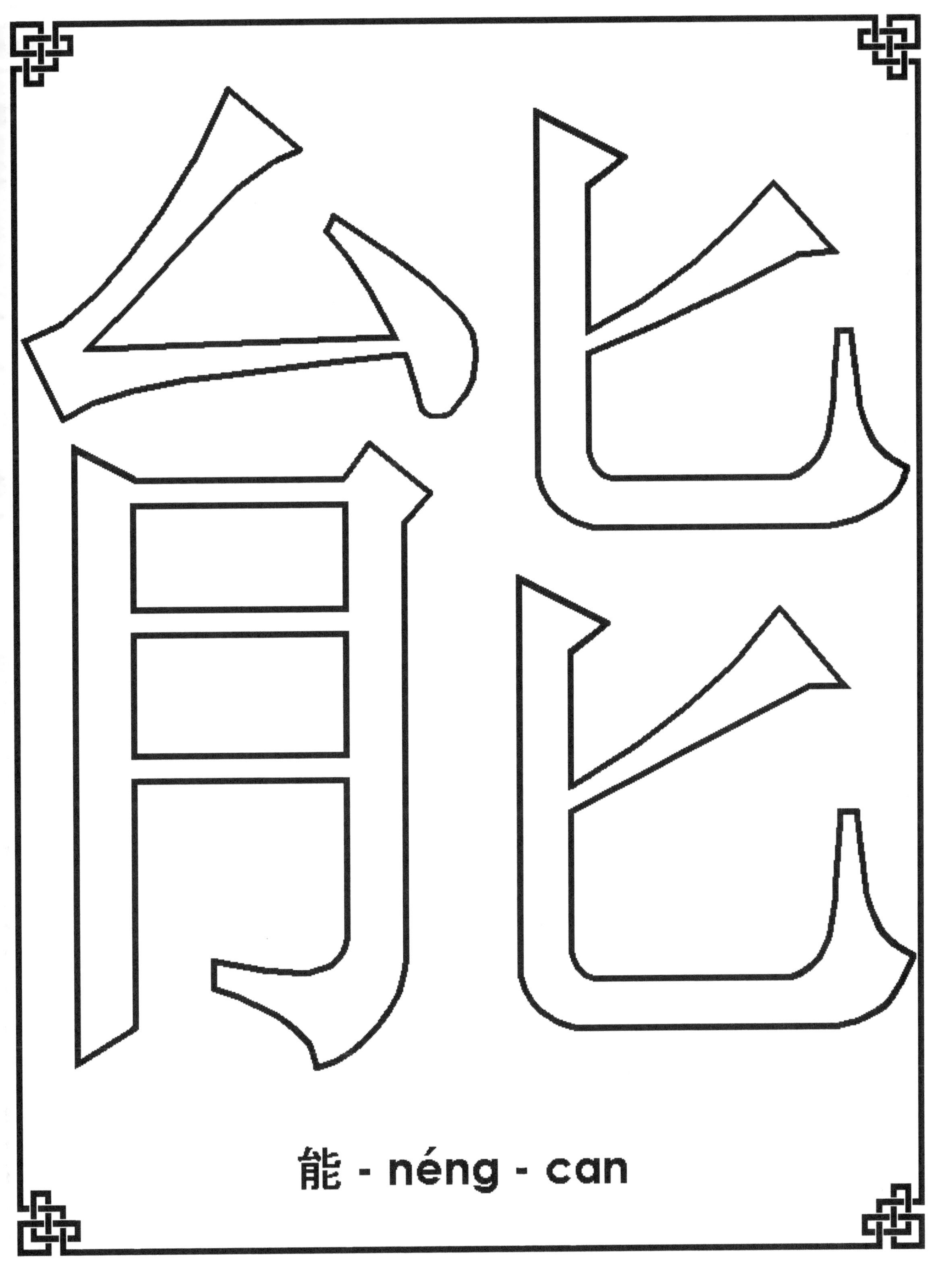

能 - néng - can

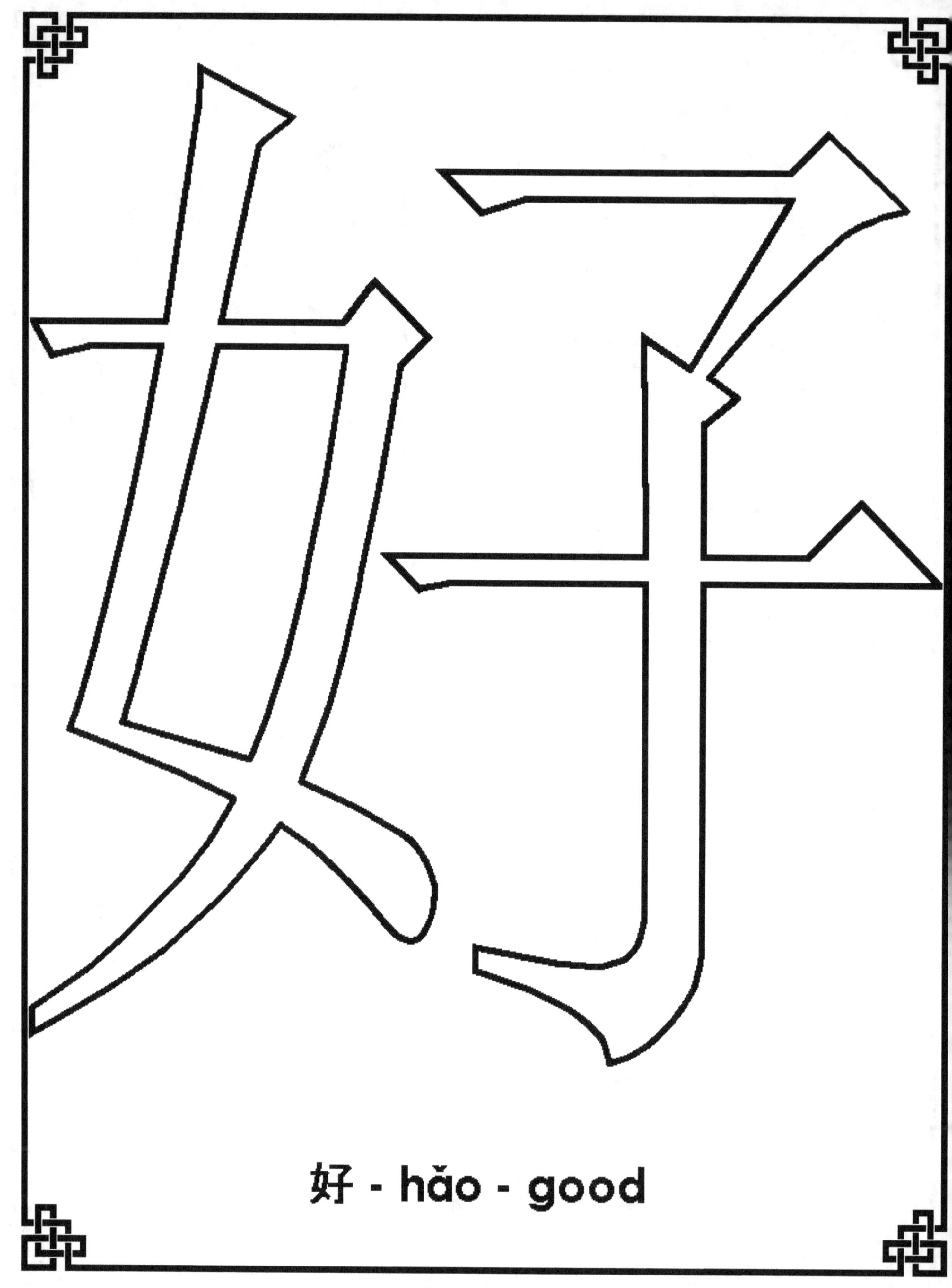

好 - hǎo - good

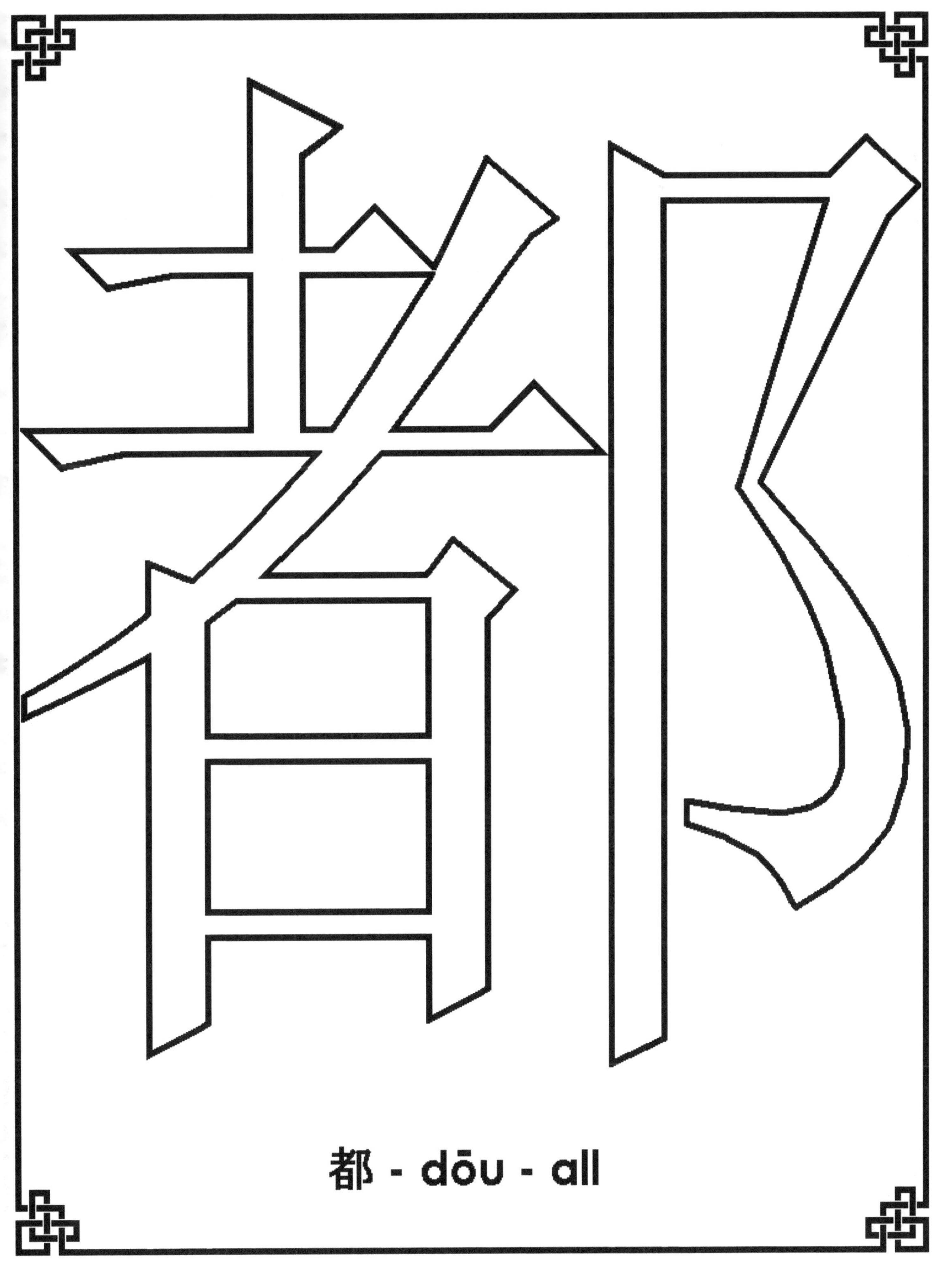

都 - dōu - all

然 - rán - correct

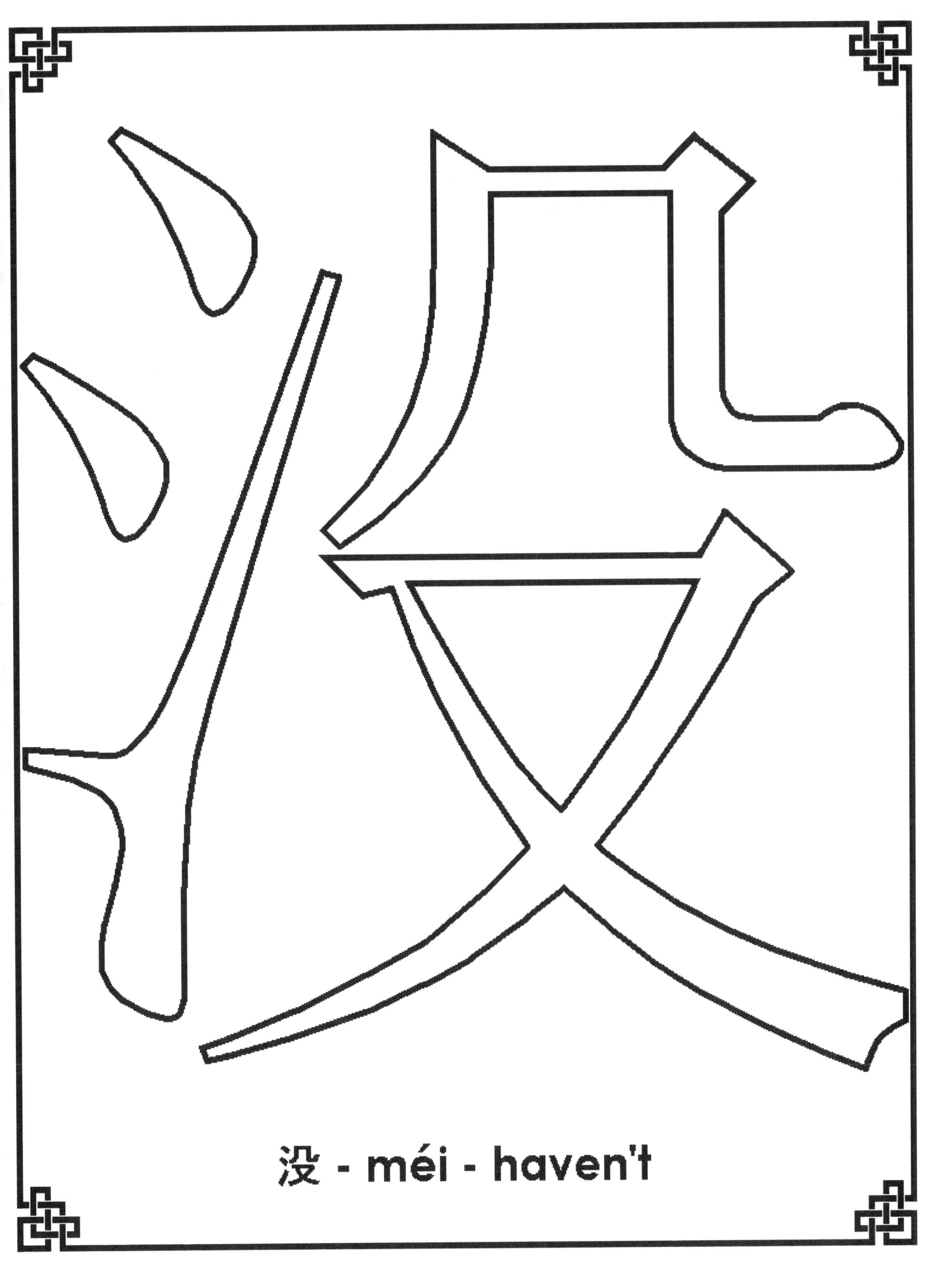

没 - méi - haven't

日 - rì - sun

于 - yú - in

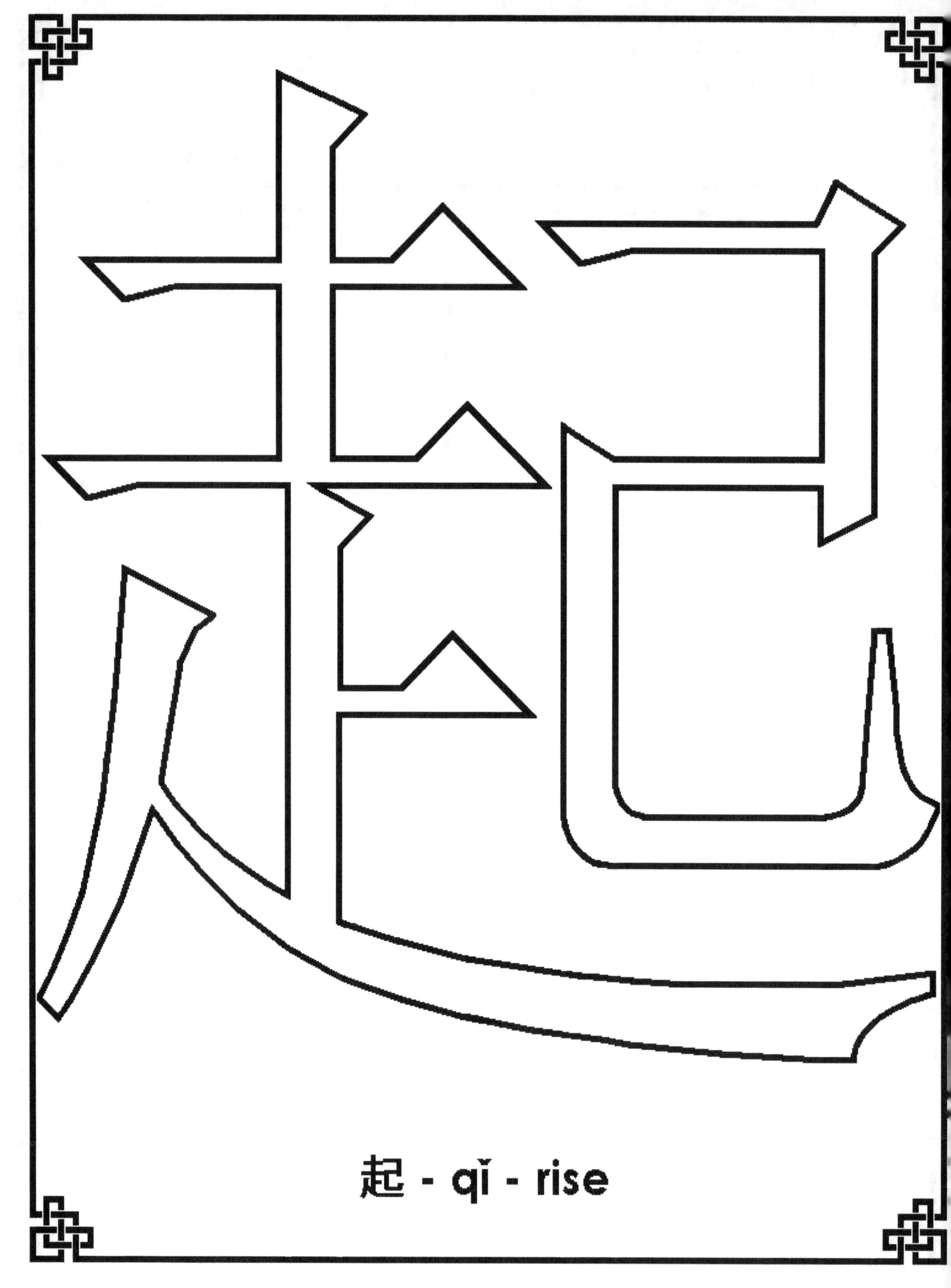

起 - qǐ - rise

还 - hái - still

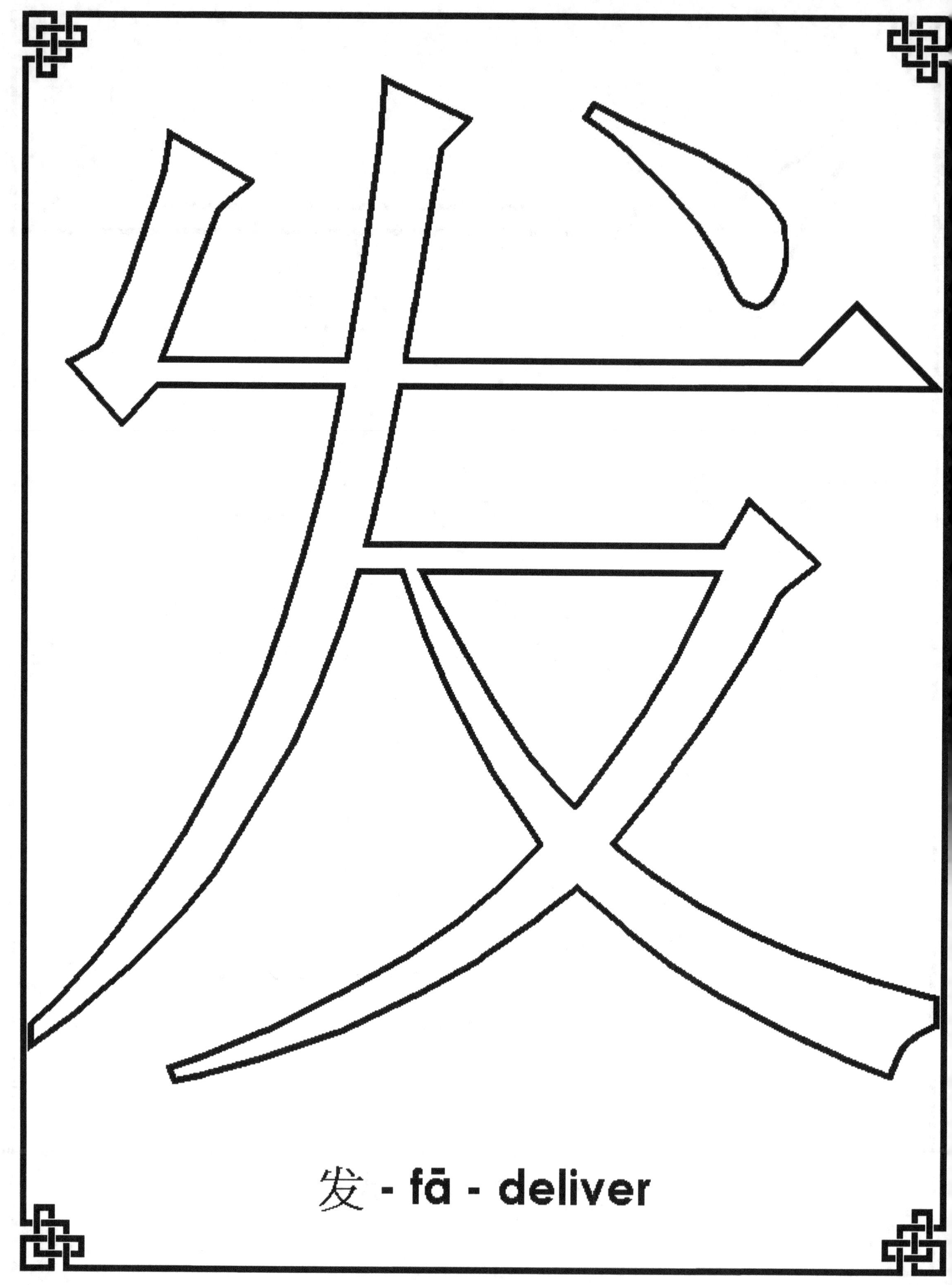

发 - fā - deliver

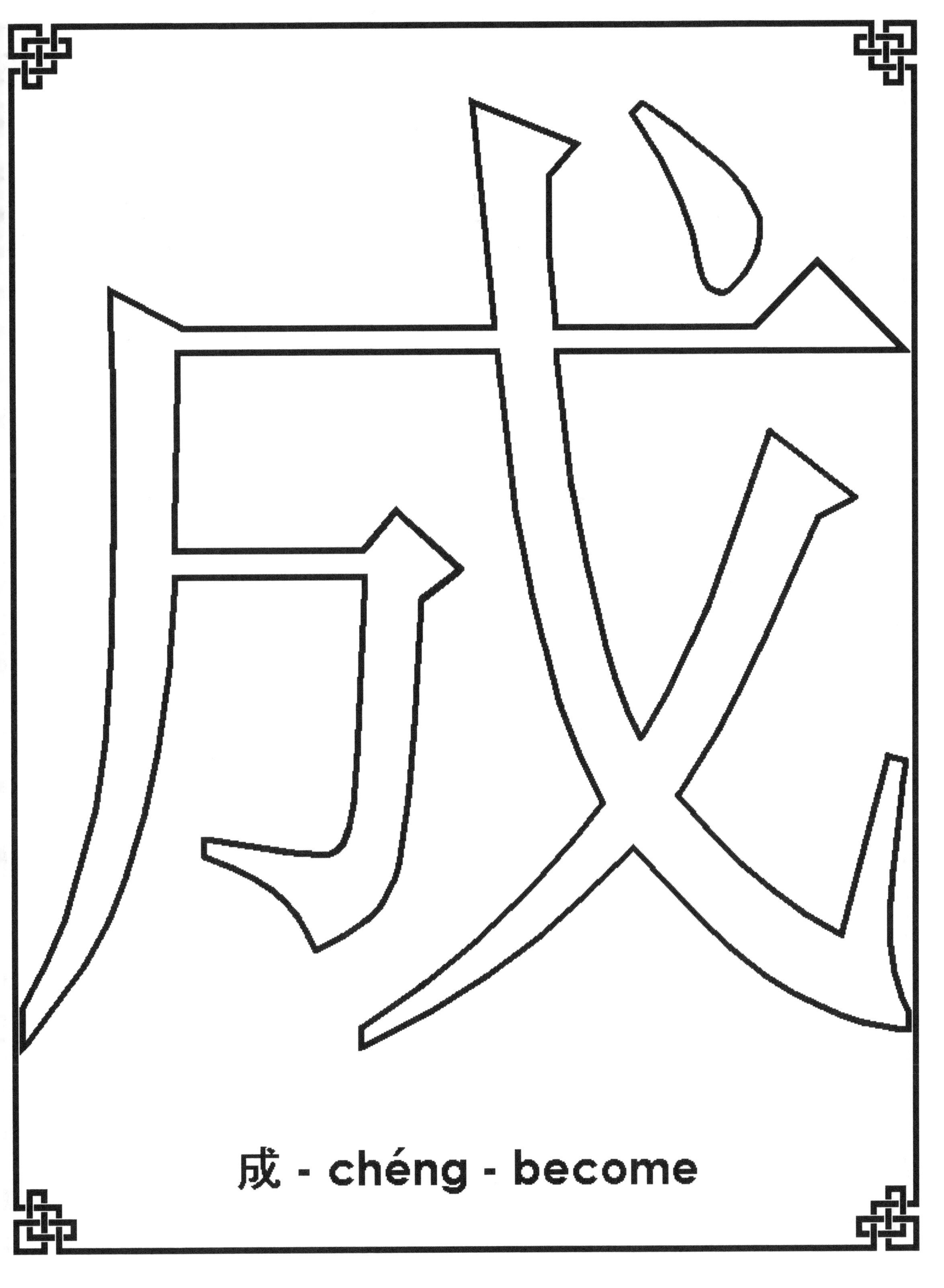

成 - chéng - become

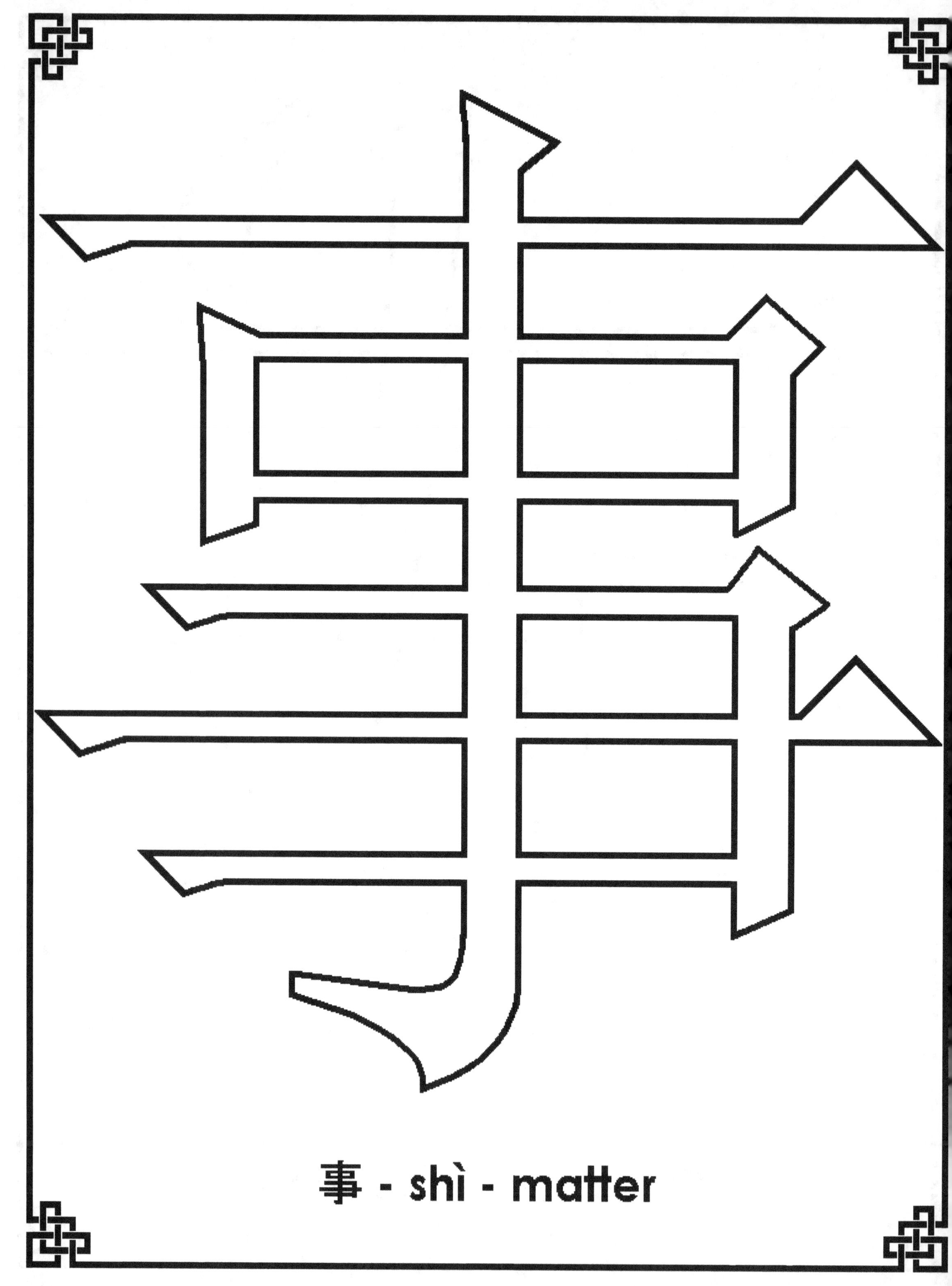

事 - shì - matter

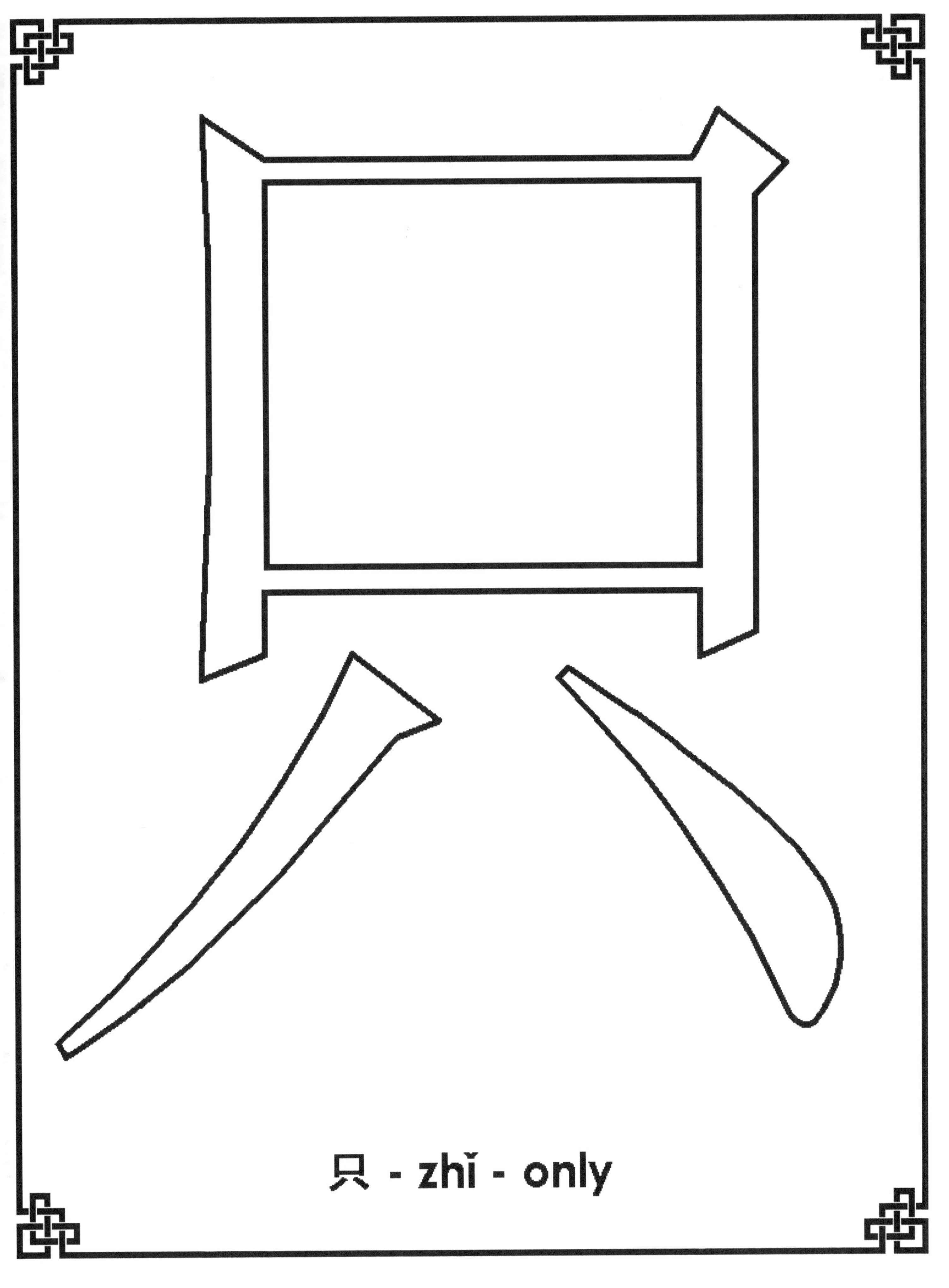

只 - zhǐ - only

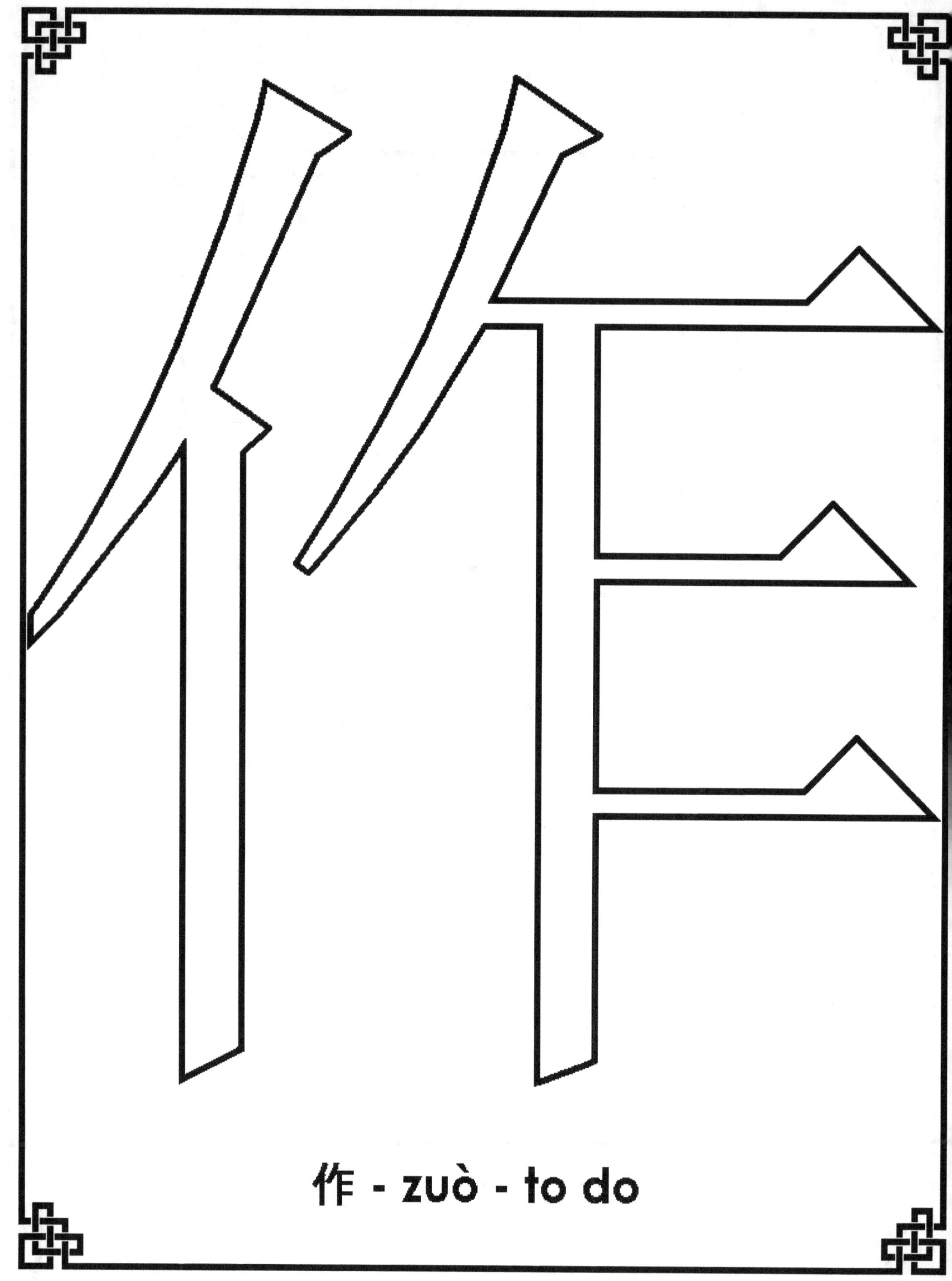

作 - zuò - to do

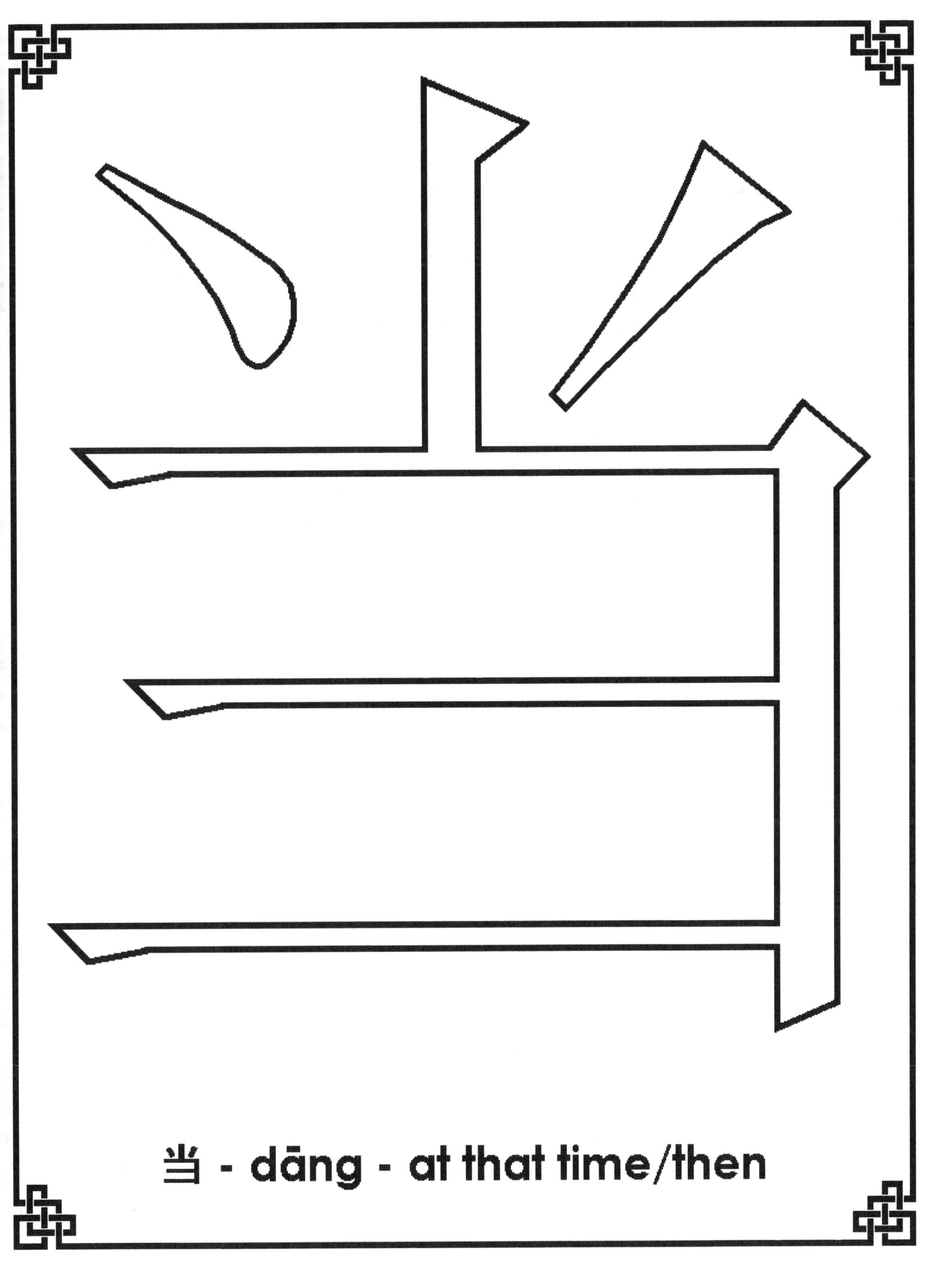

当 - dāng - at that time/then

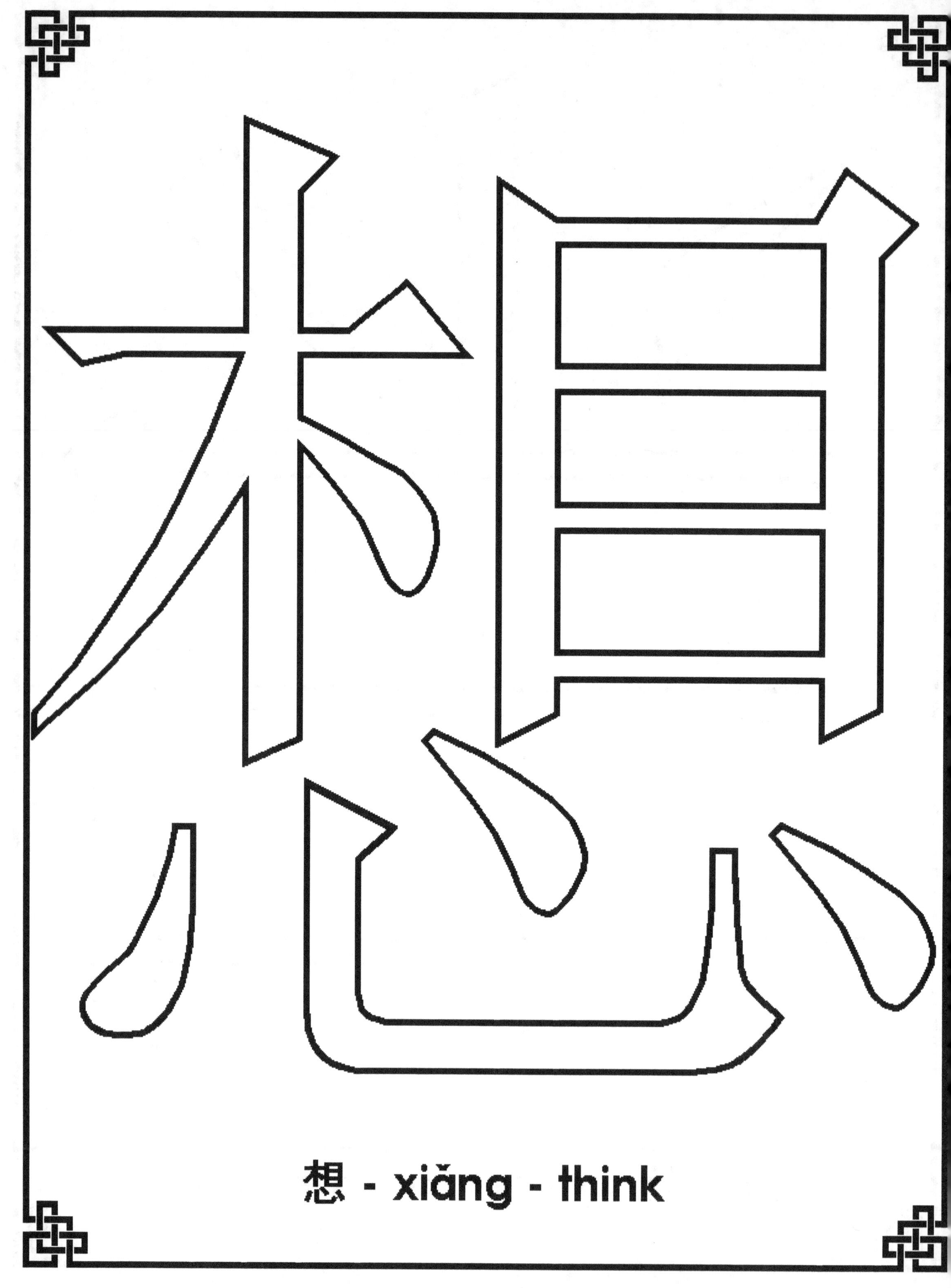

想 - xiǎng - think

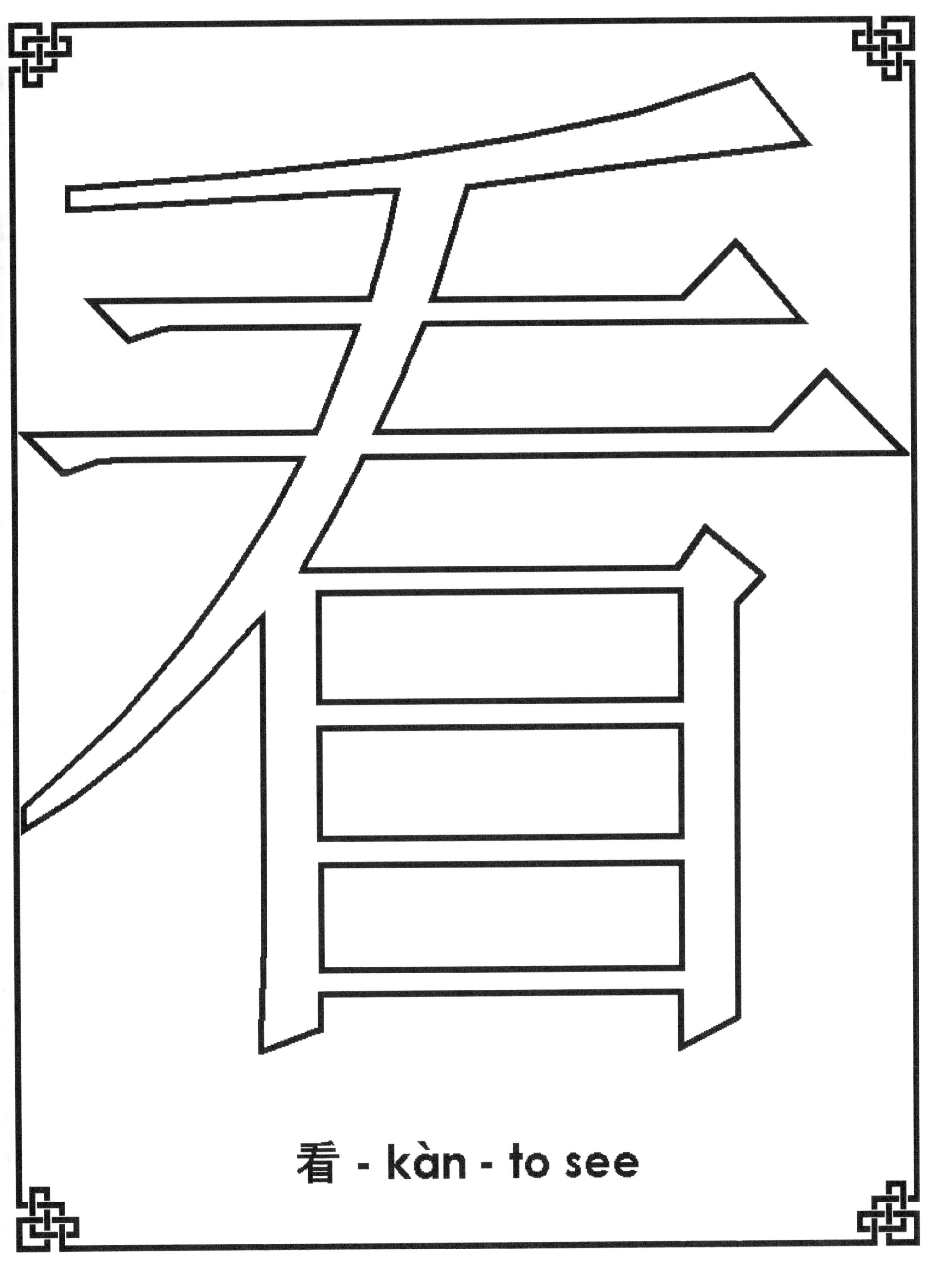

看 - kàn - to see

文 - wén - language

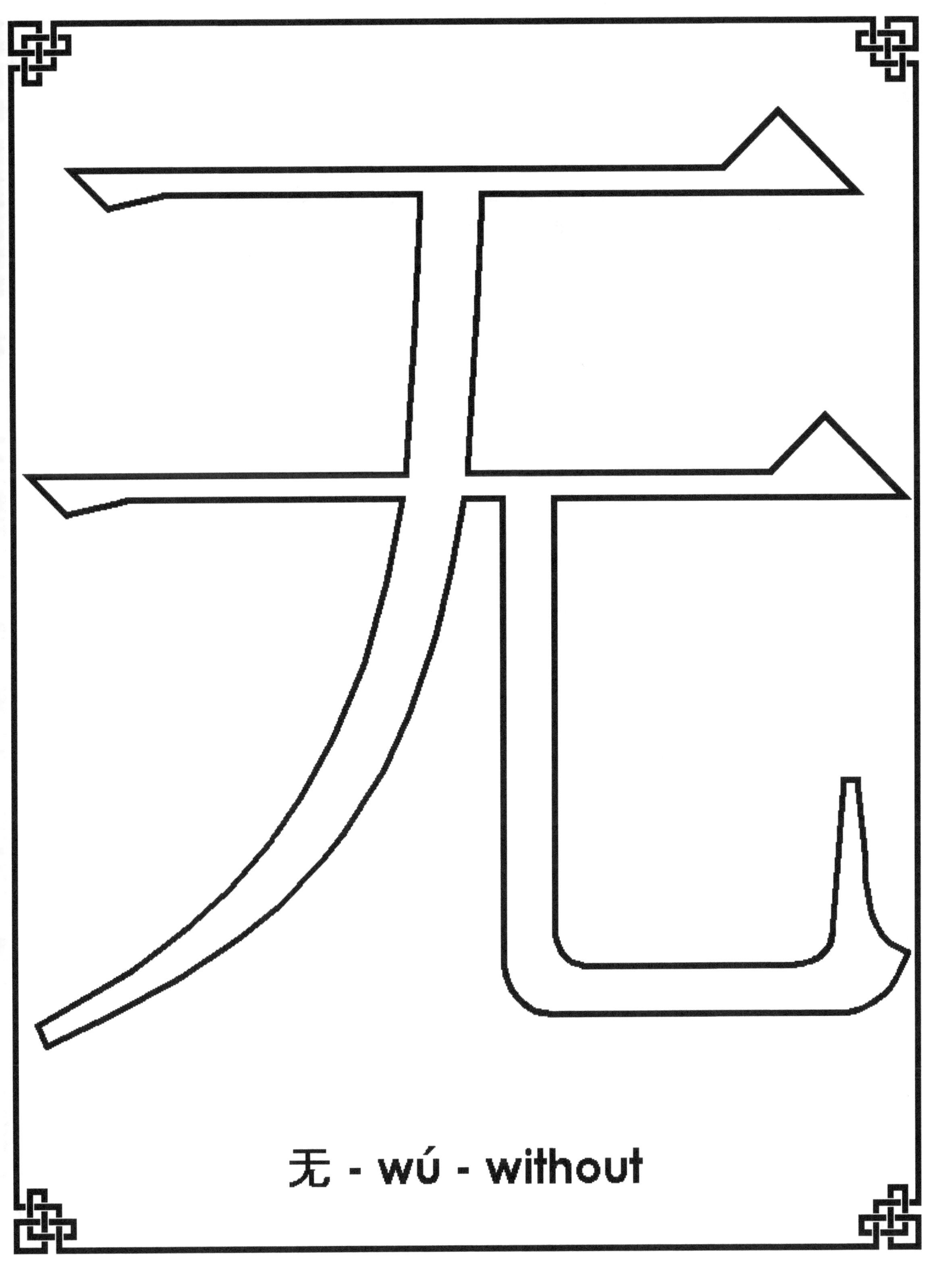

无 - wú - without

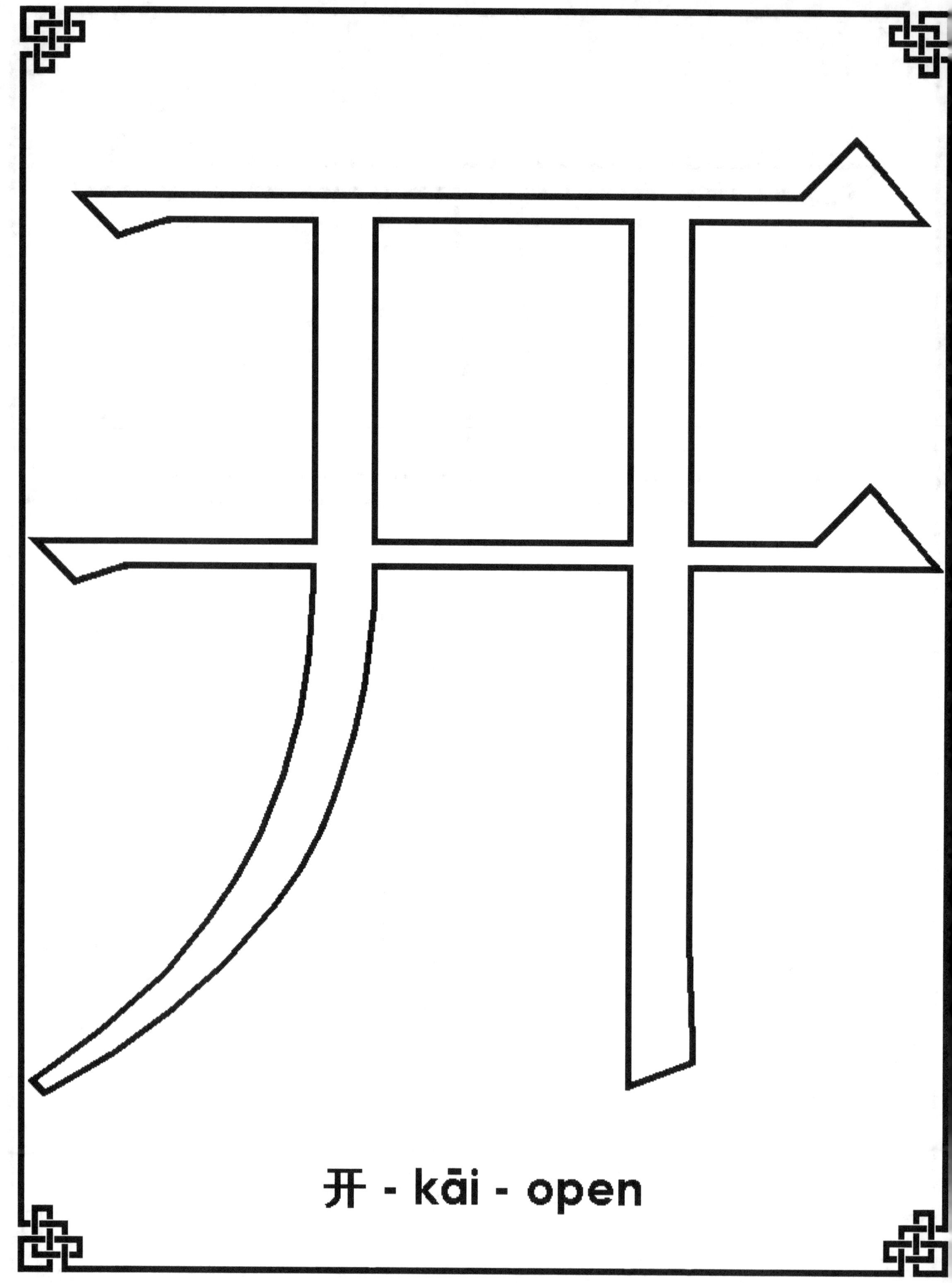

开 - kāi - open

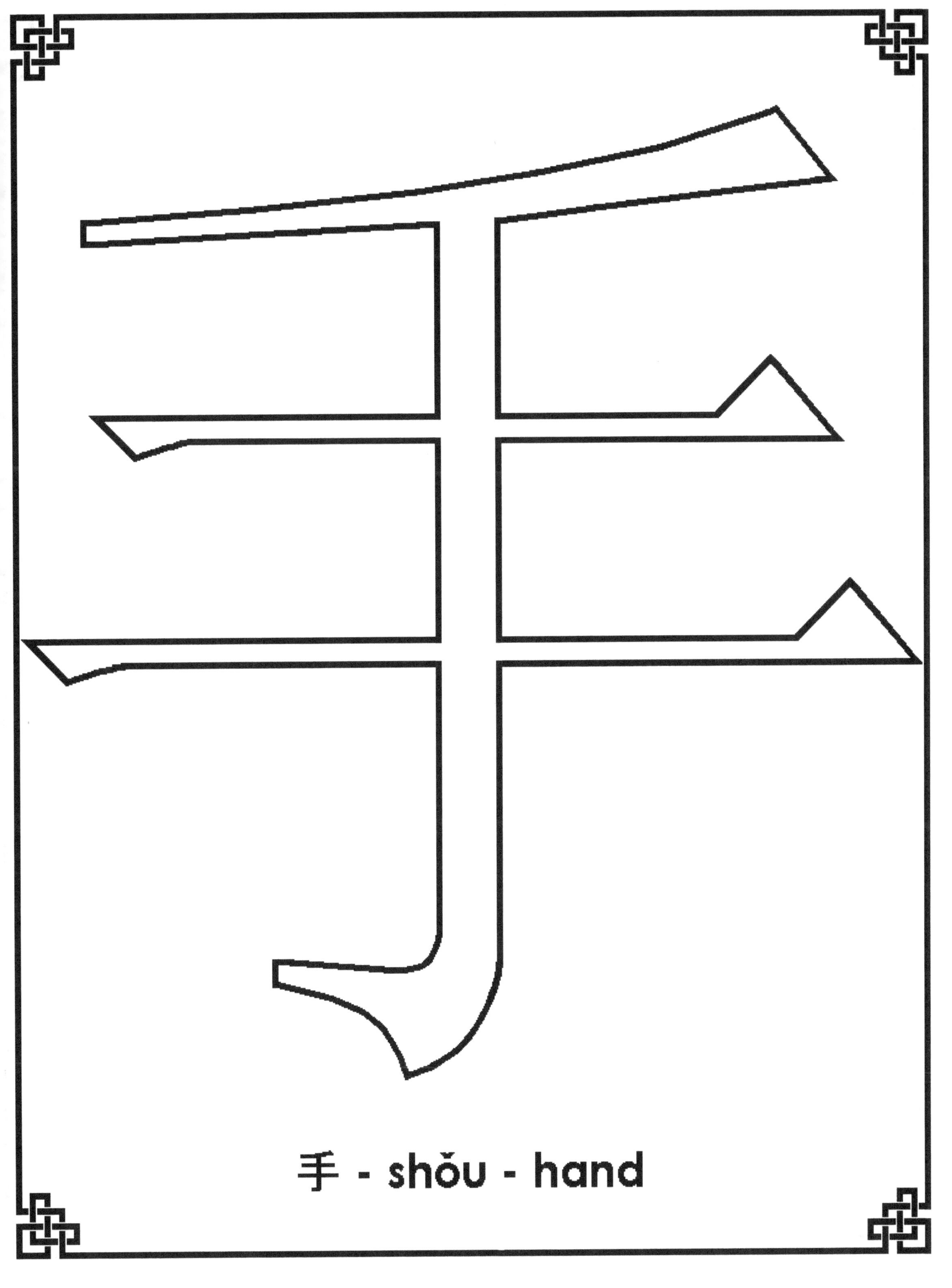

手 - shǒu - hand

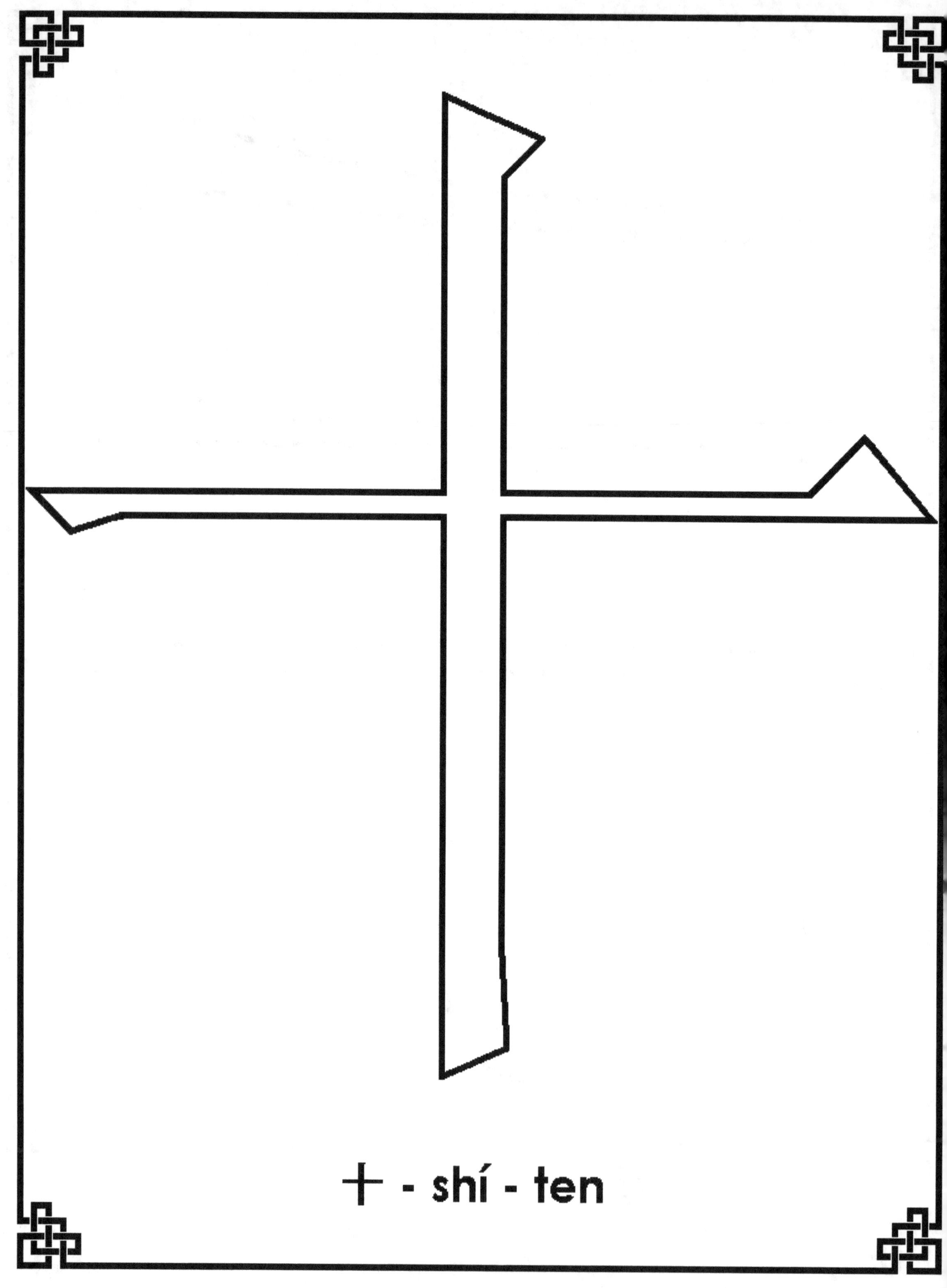

✝ - shí - ten

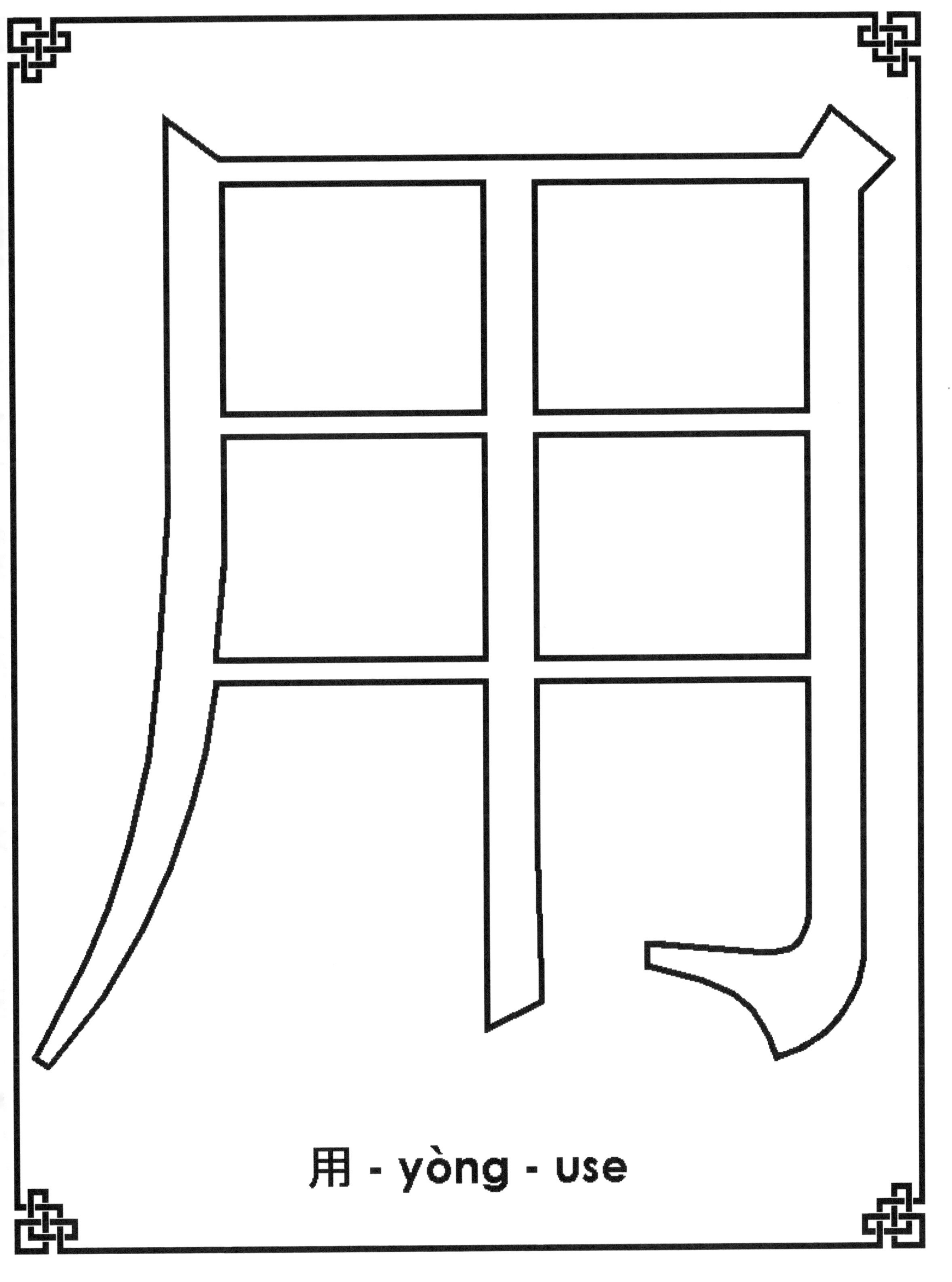

用 - yòng - use

主 - zhǔ - lord

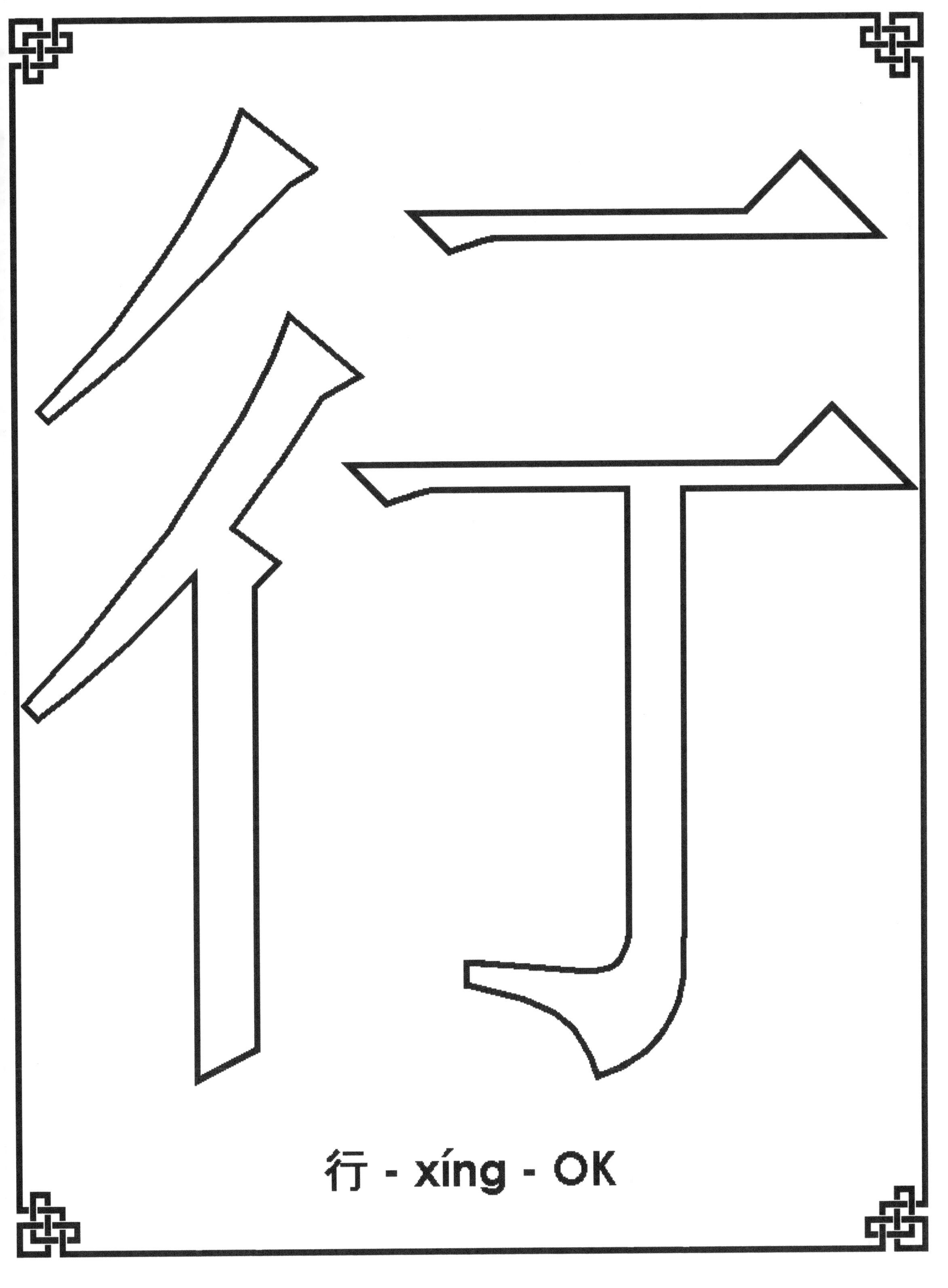

行 - xíng - OK

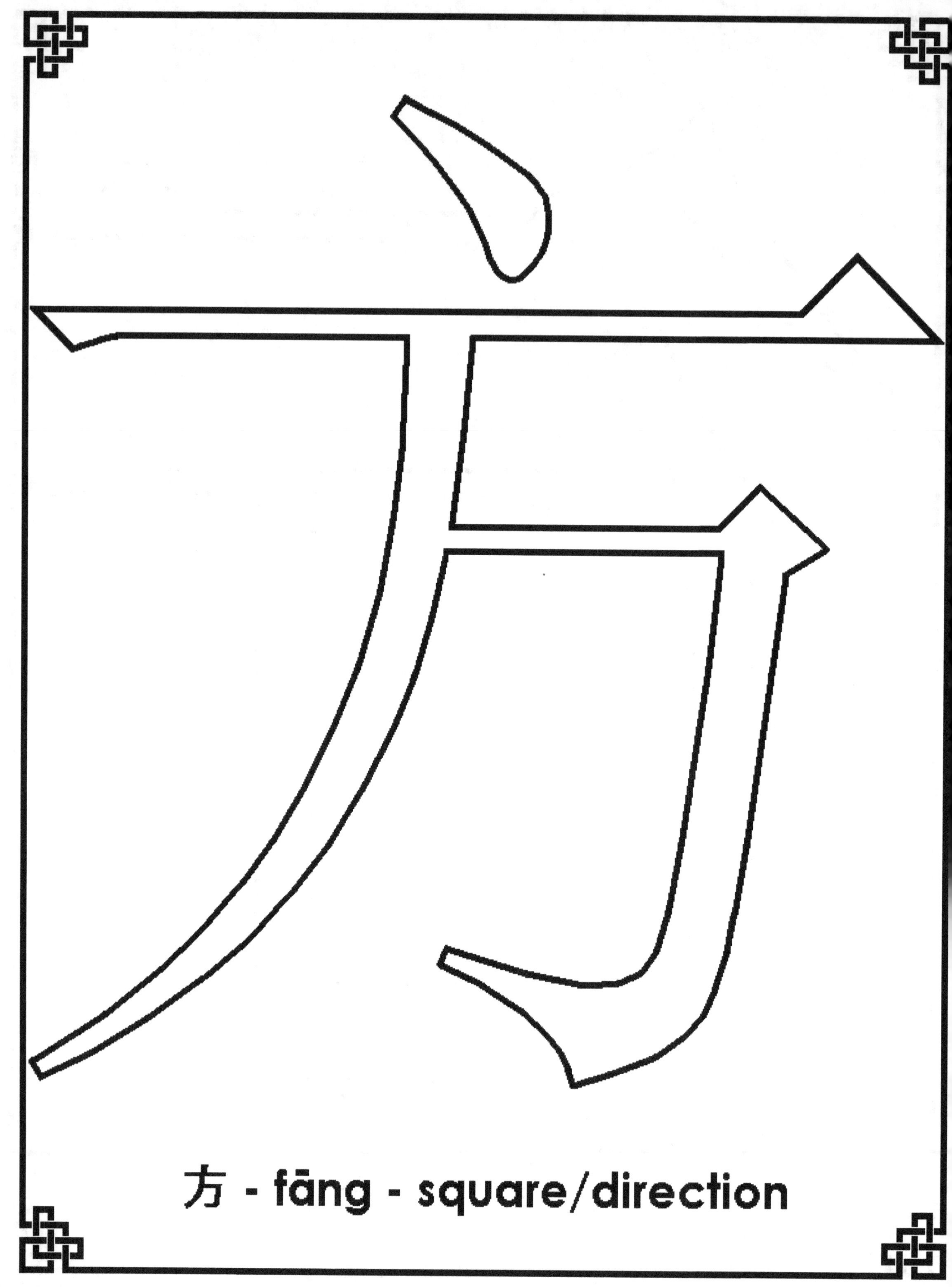

方 - fāng - square/direction

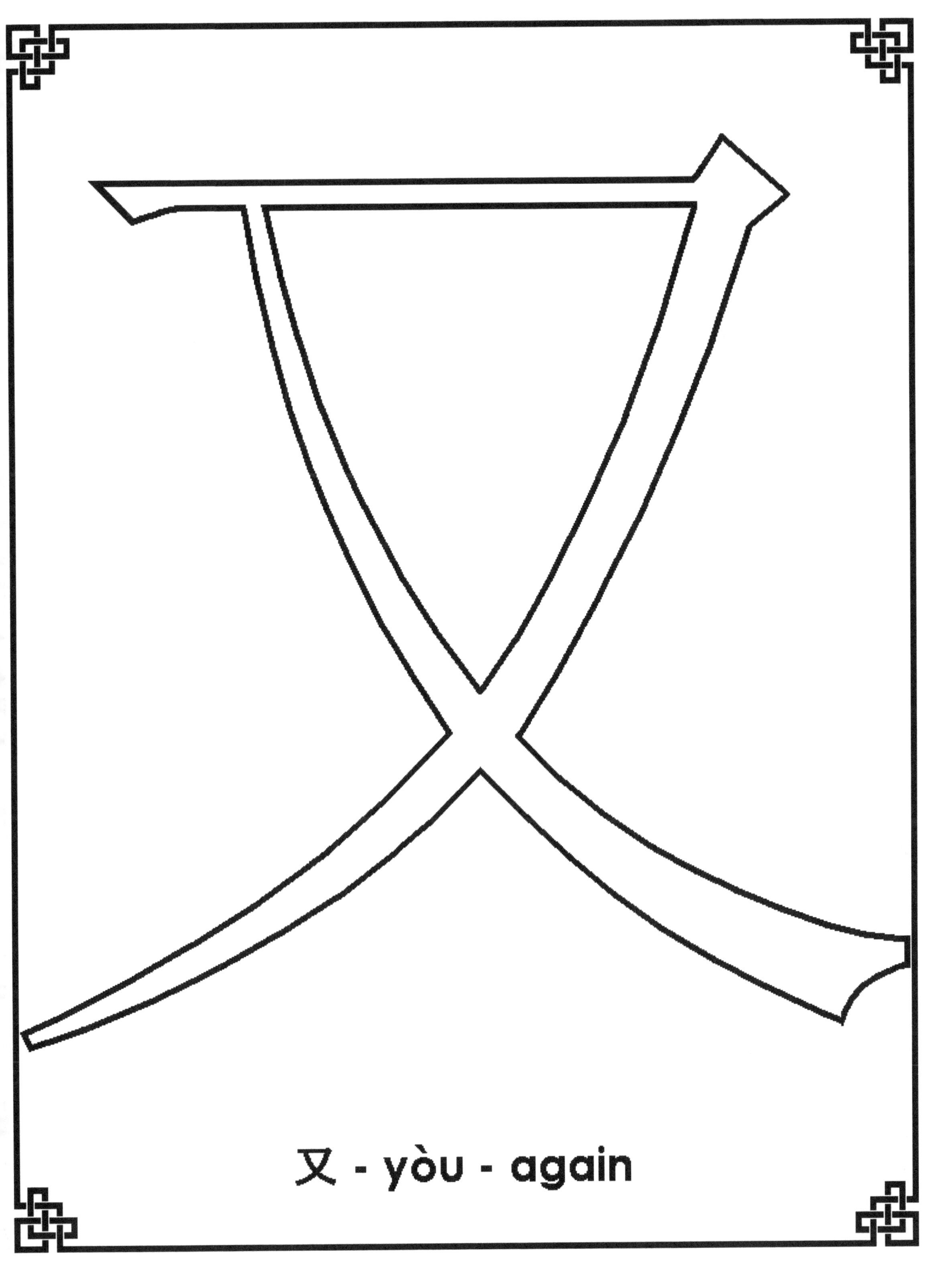

又 - yòu - again

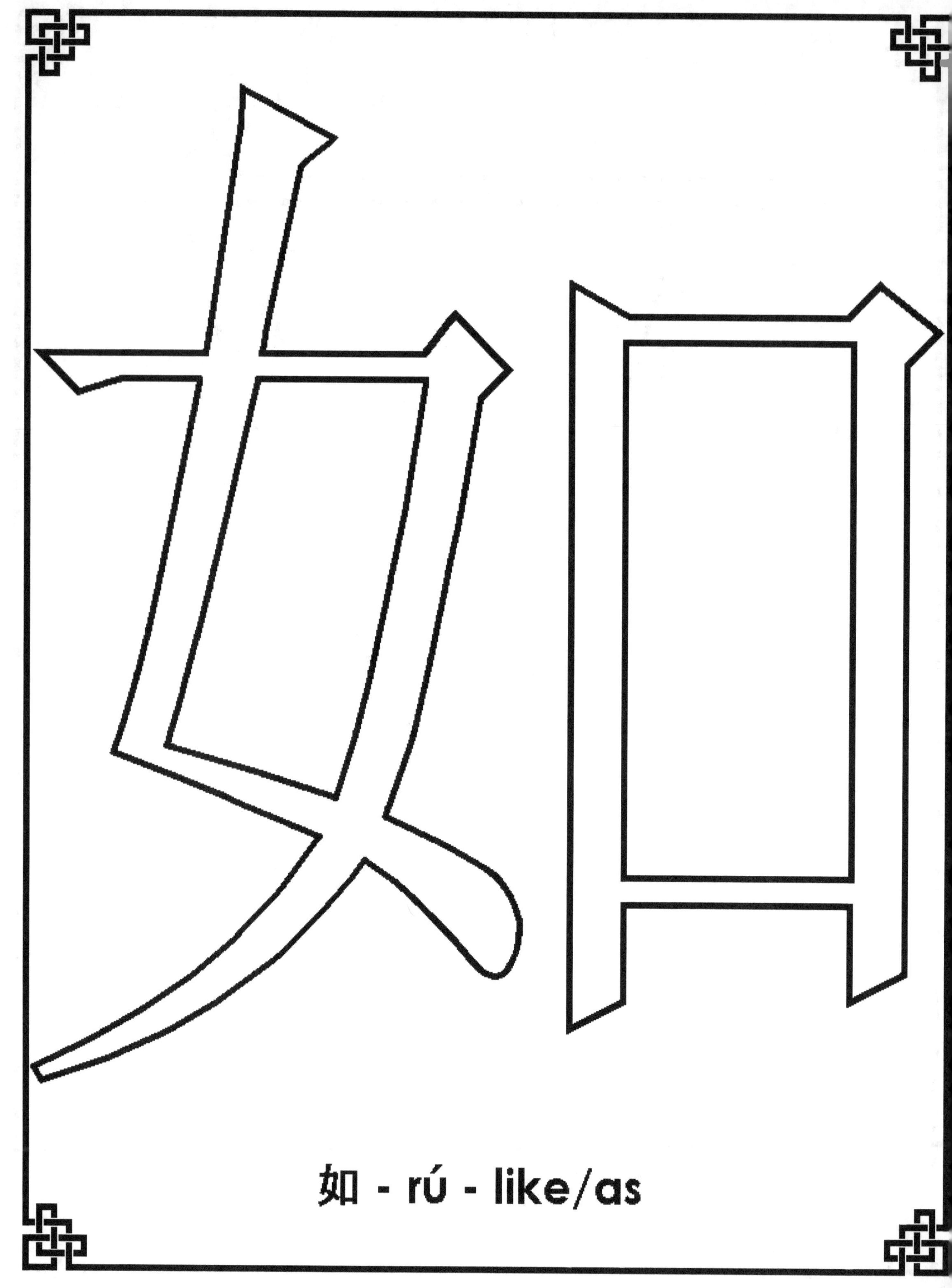

如 - rú - like/as

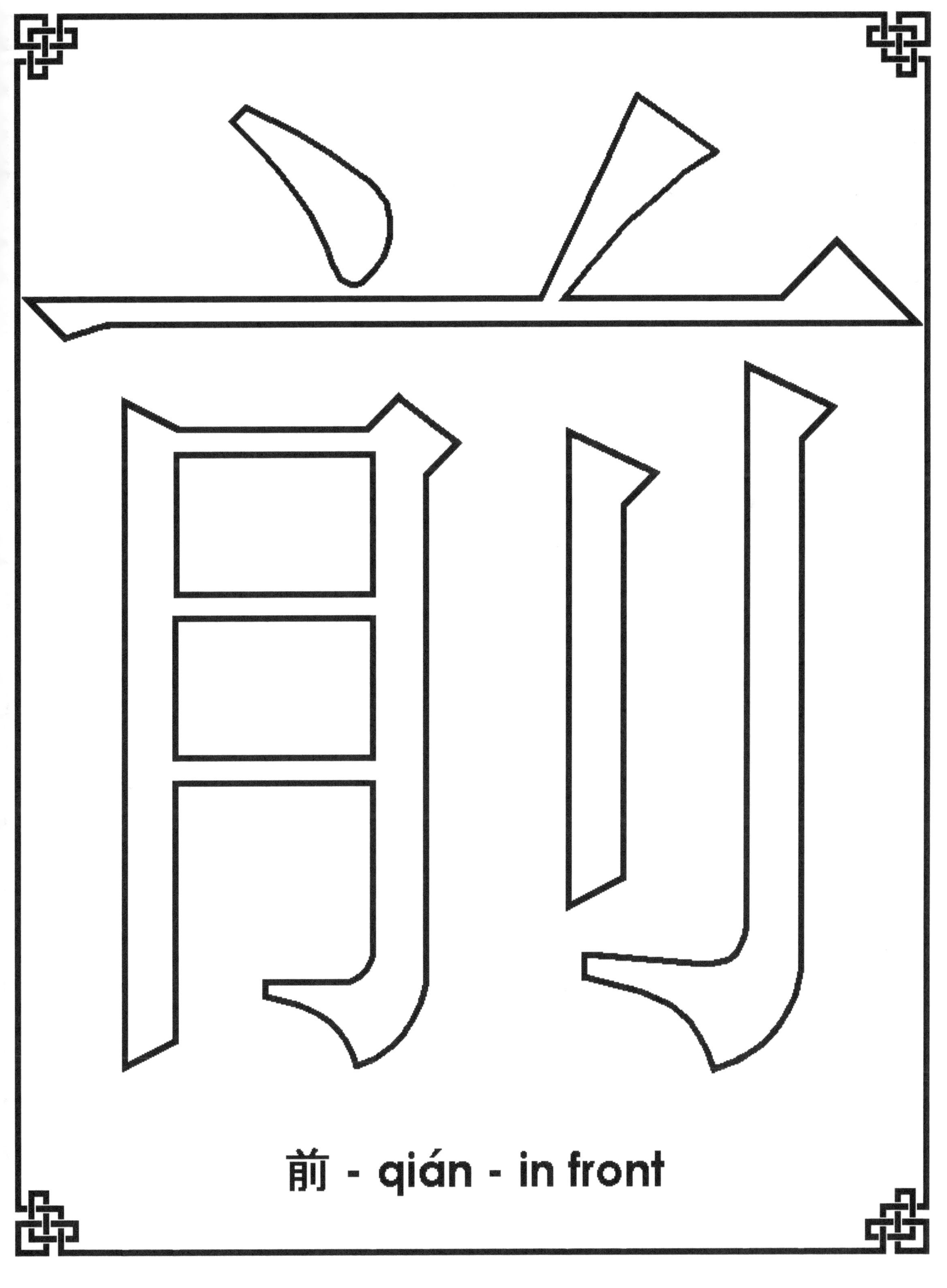

前 - qián - in front

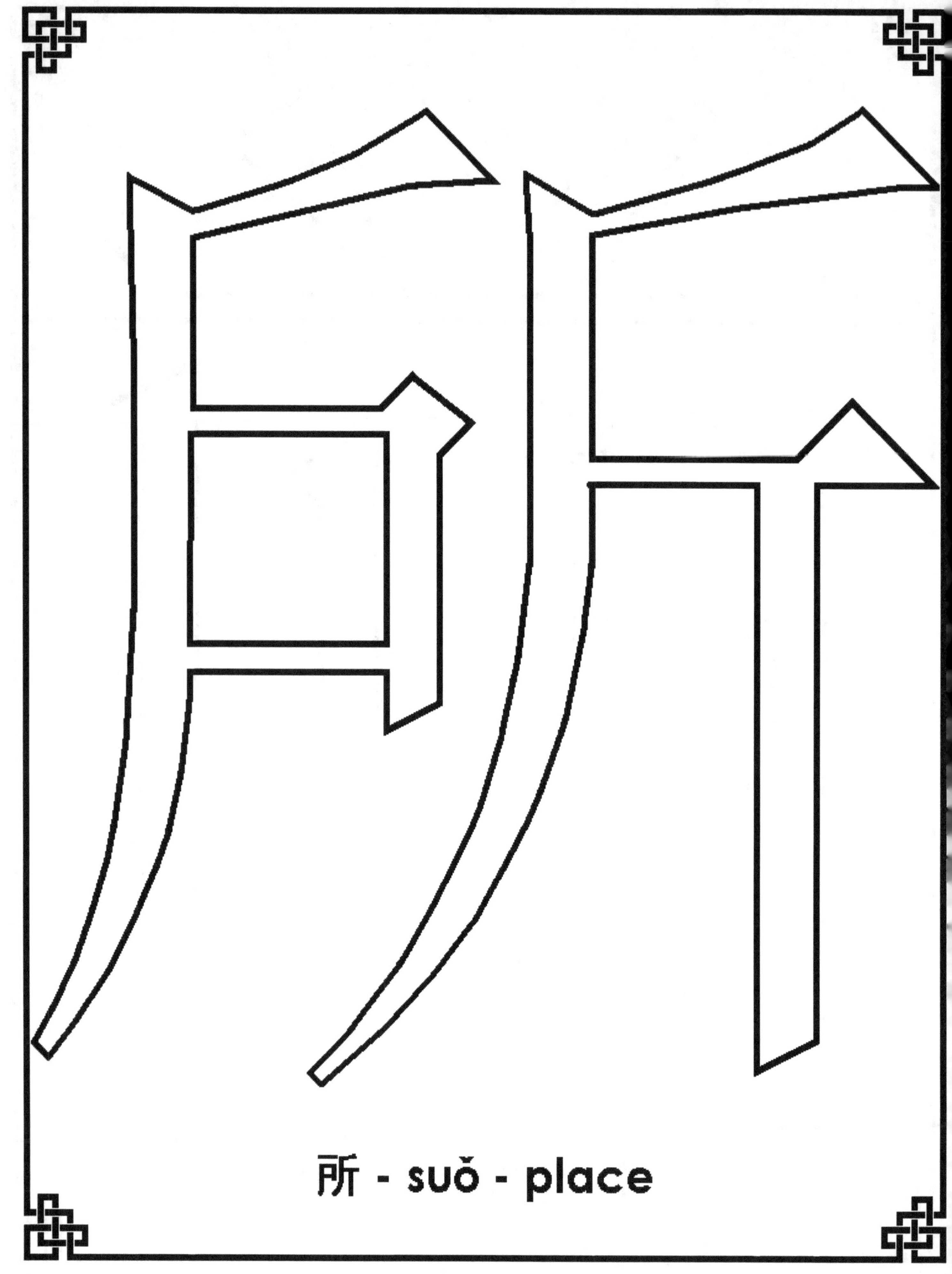

所 - suǒ - place

本 - běn - origin

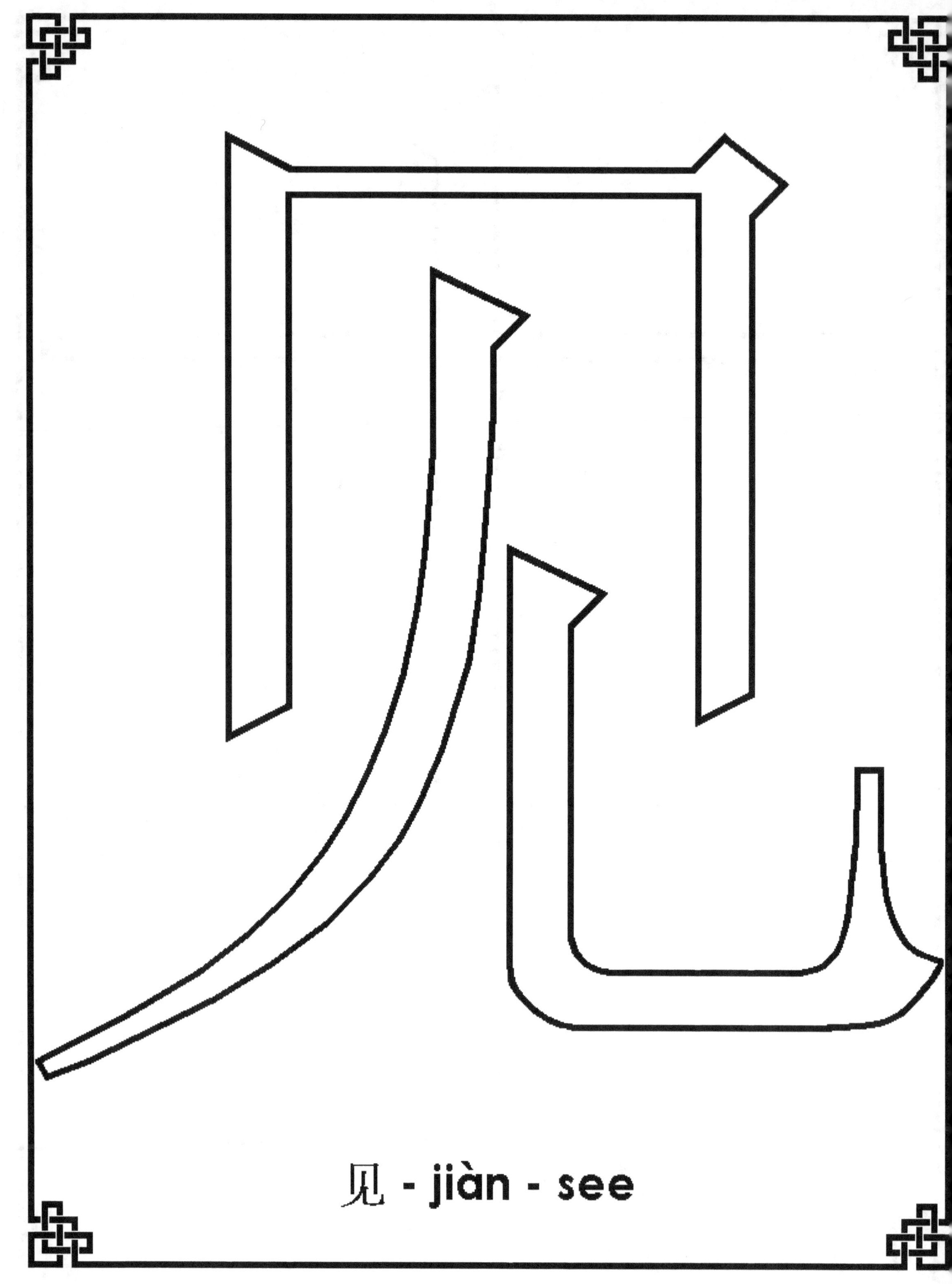

见 - jiàn - see

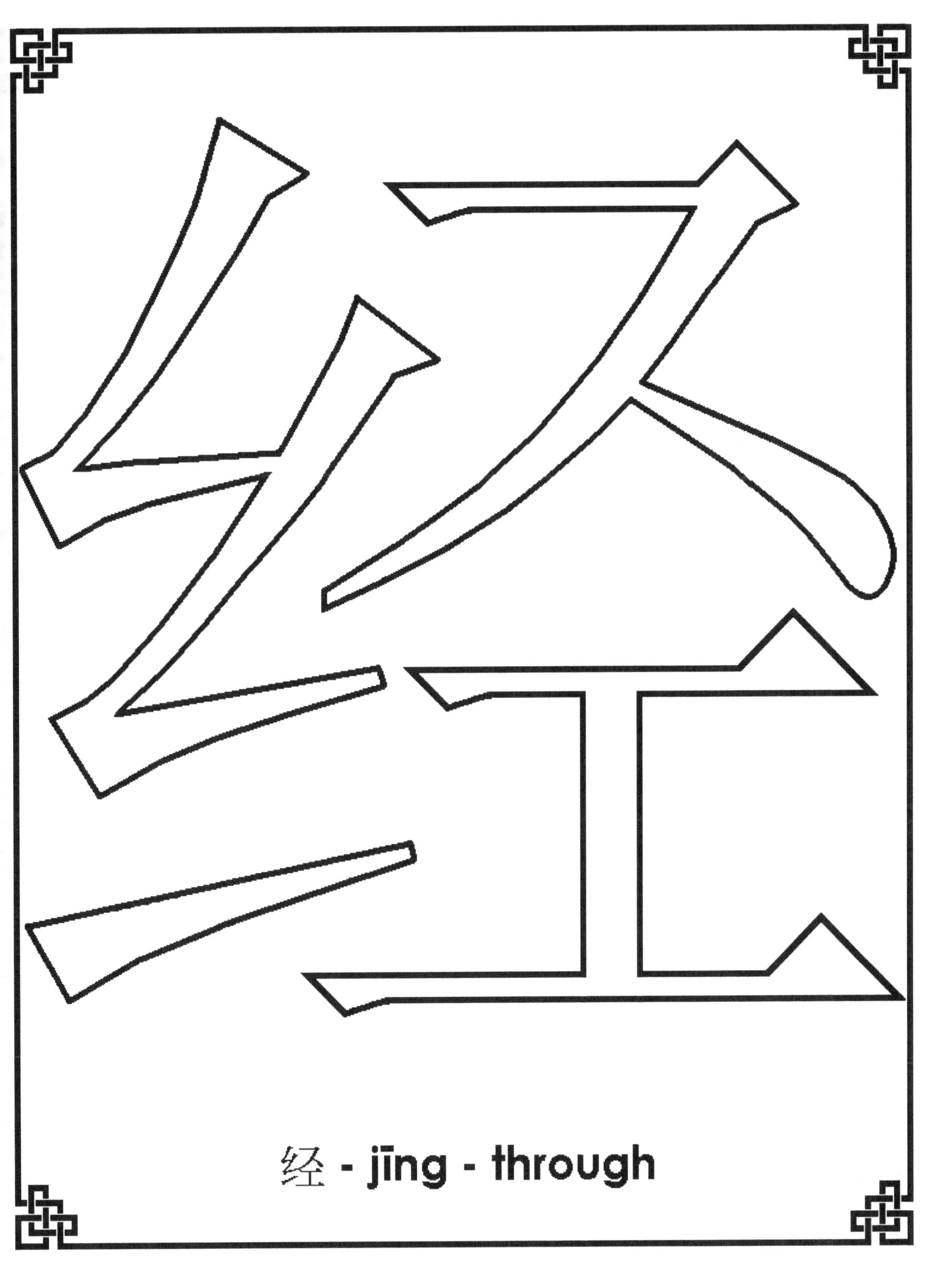

经 - jīng - through

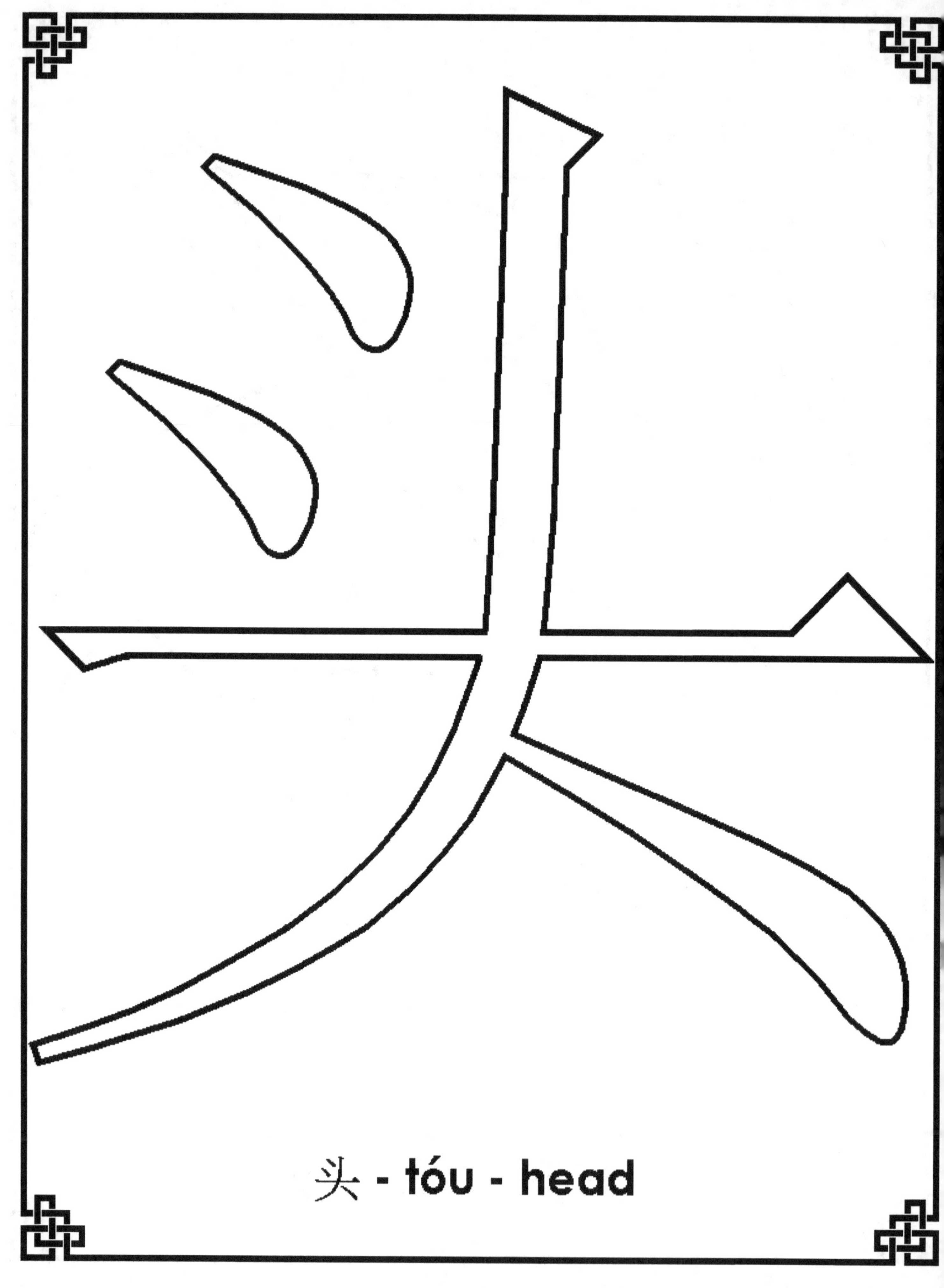

头 - tóu - head

面 - miàn - face

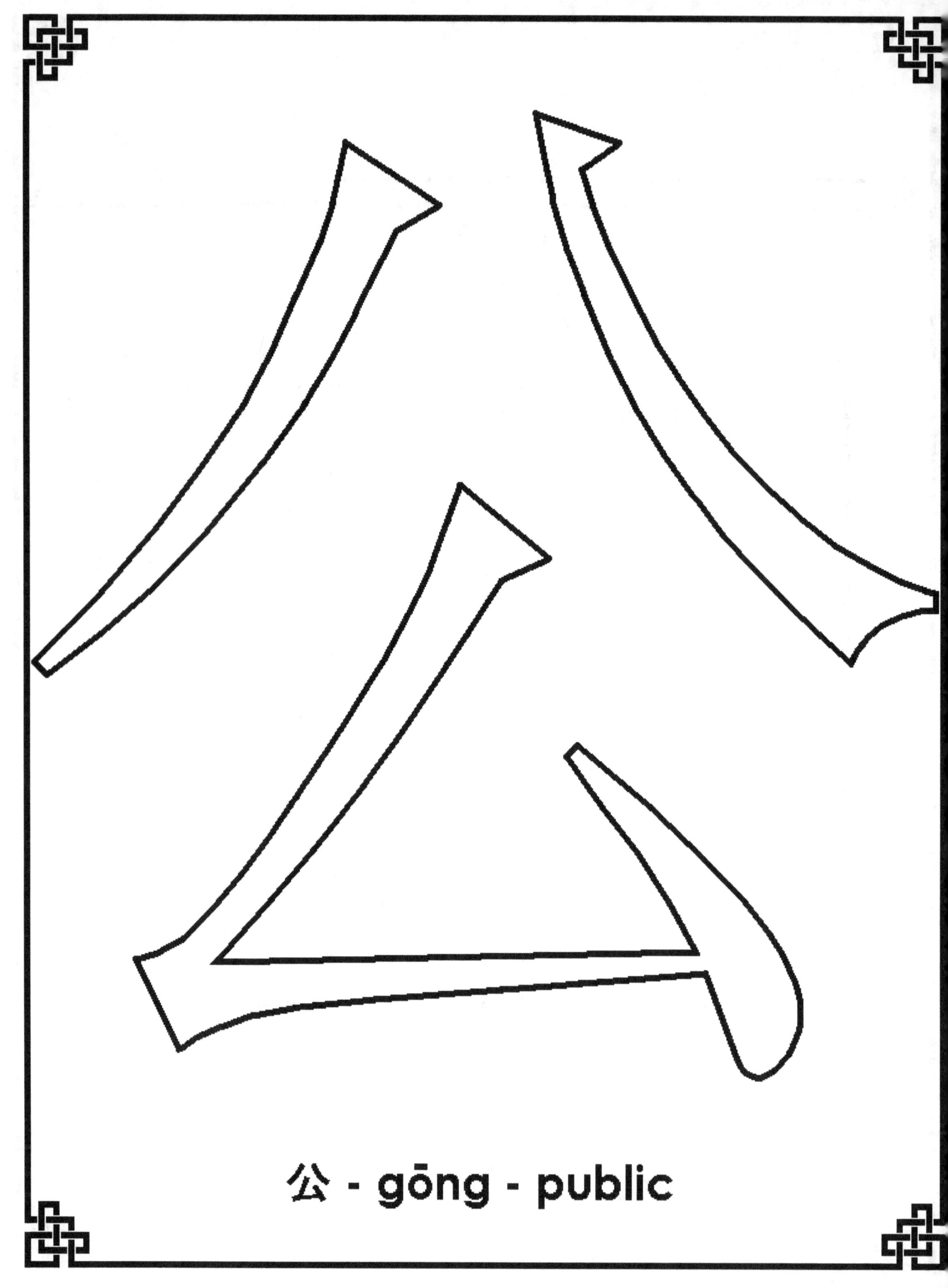

公 - gōng - public

同 - tóng - same

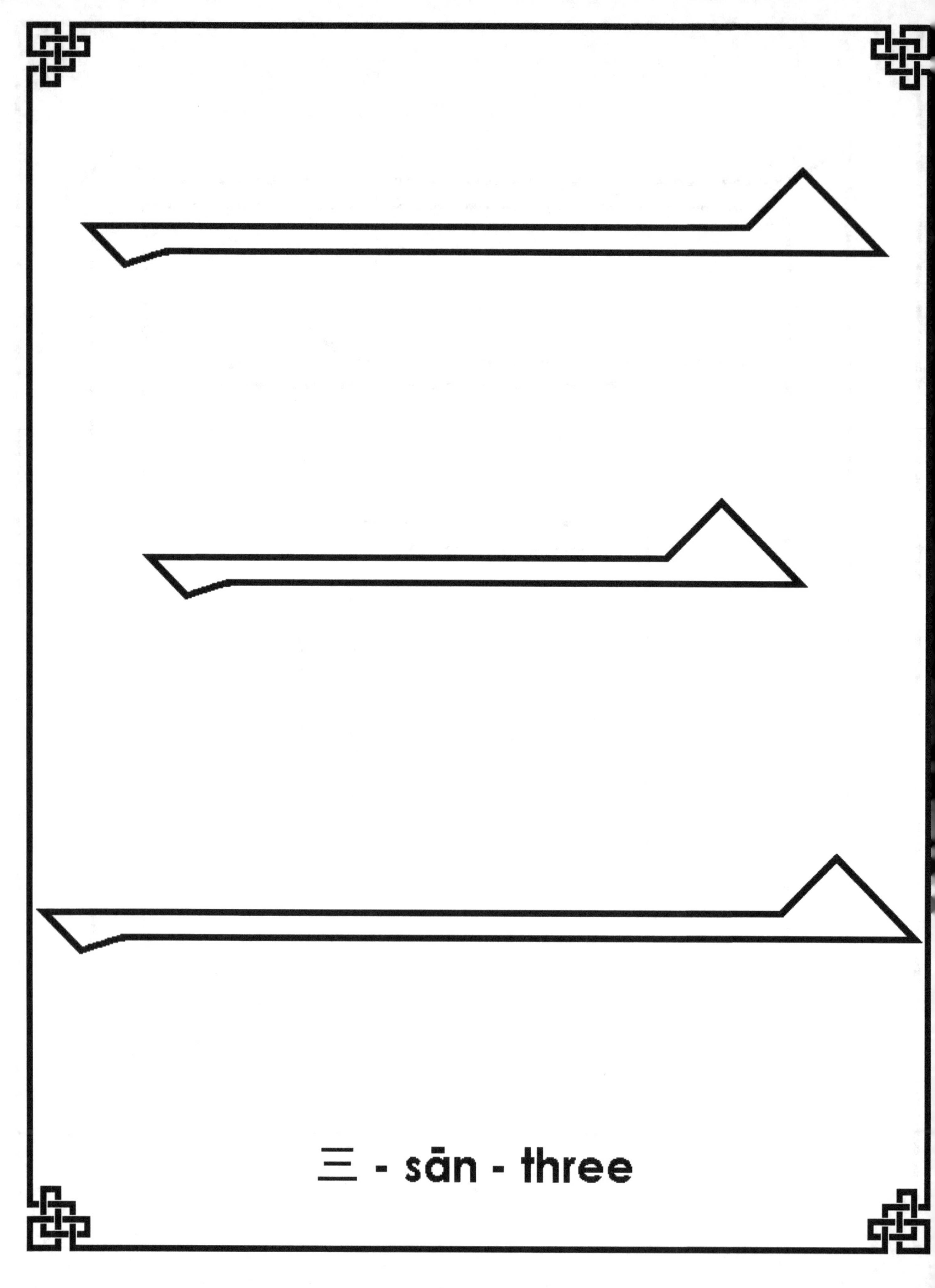

三 - sān - three

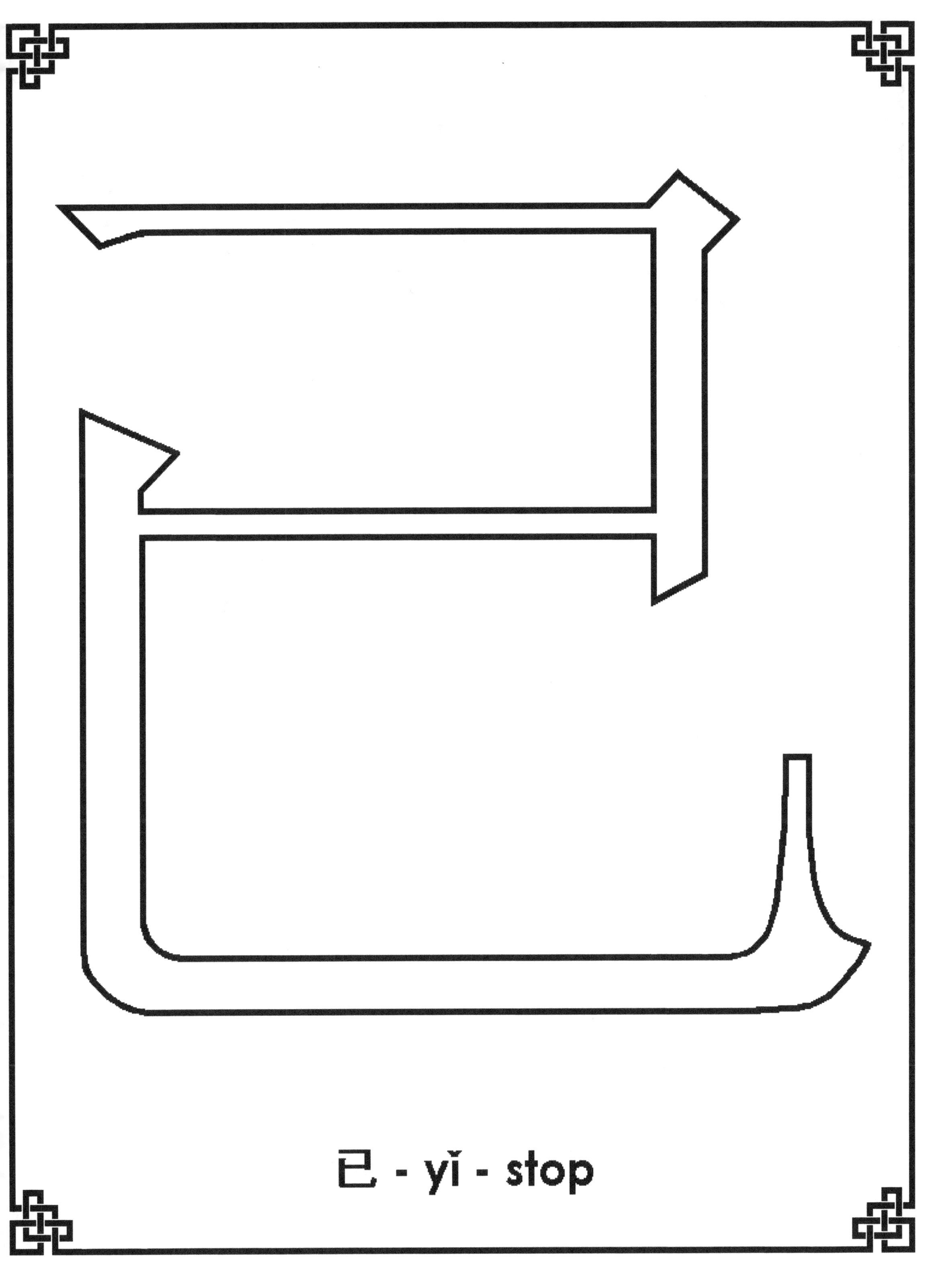

已 - yǐ - stop

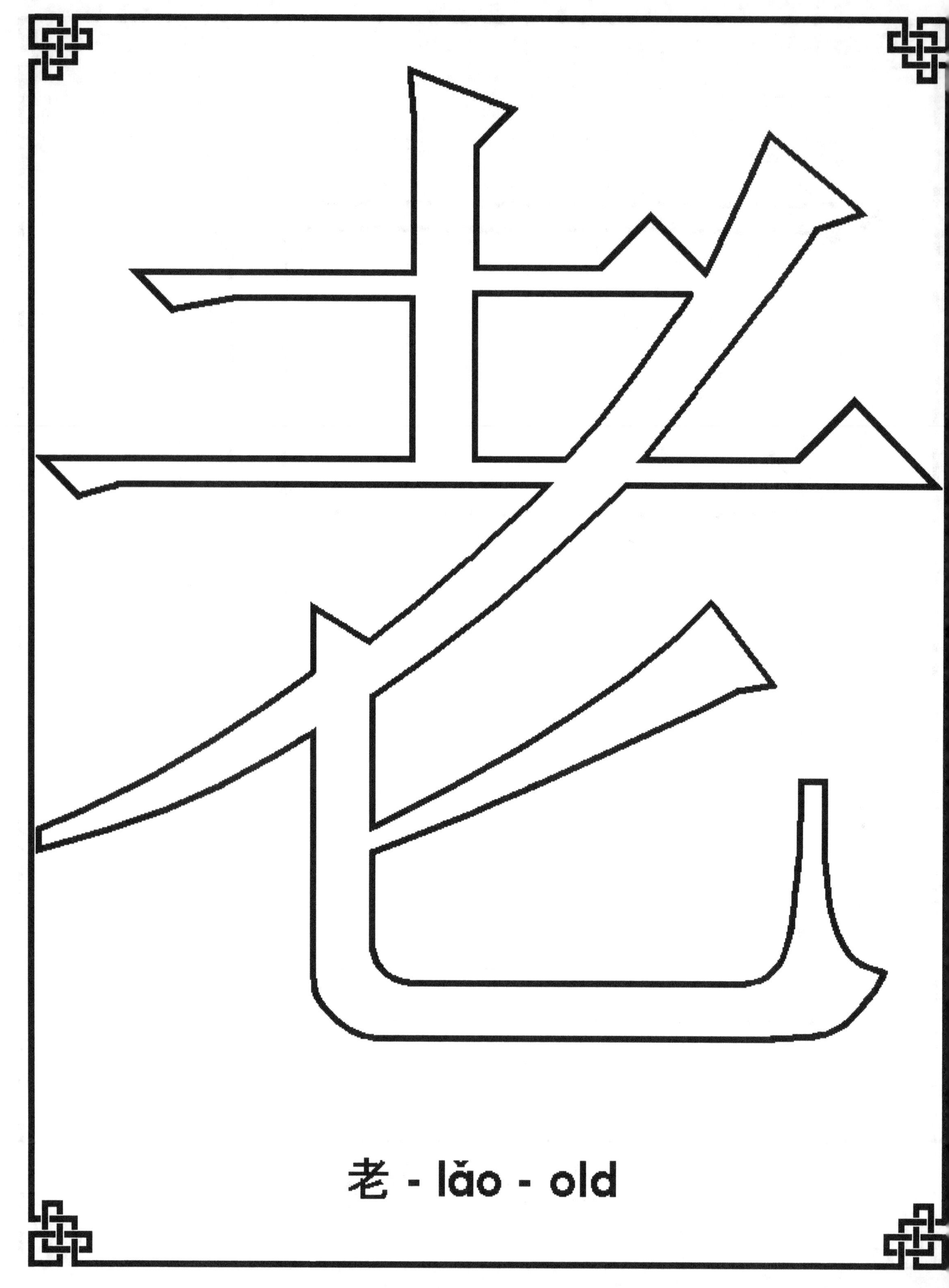

老 - lǎo - old

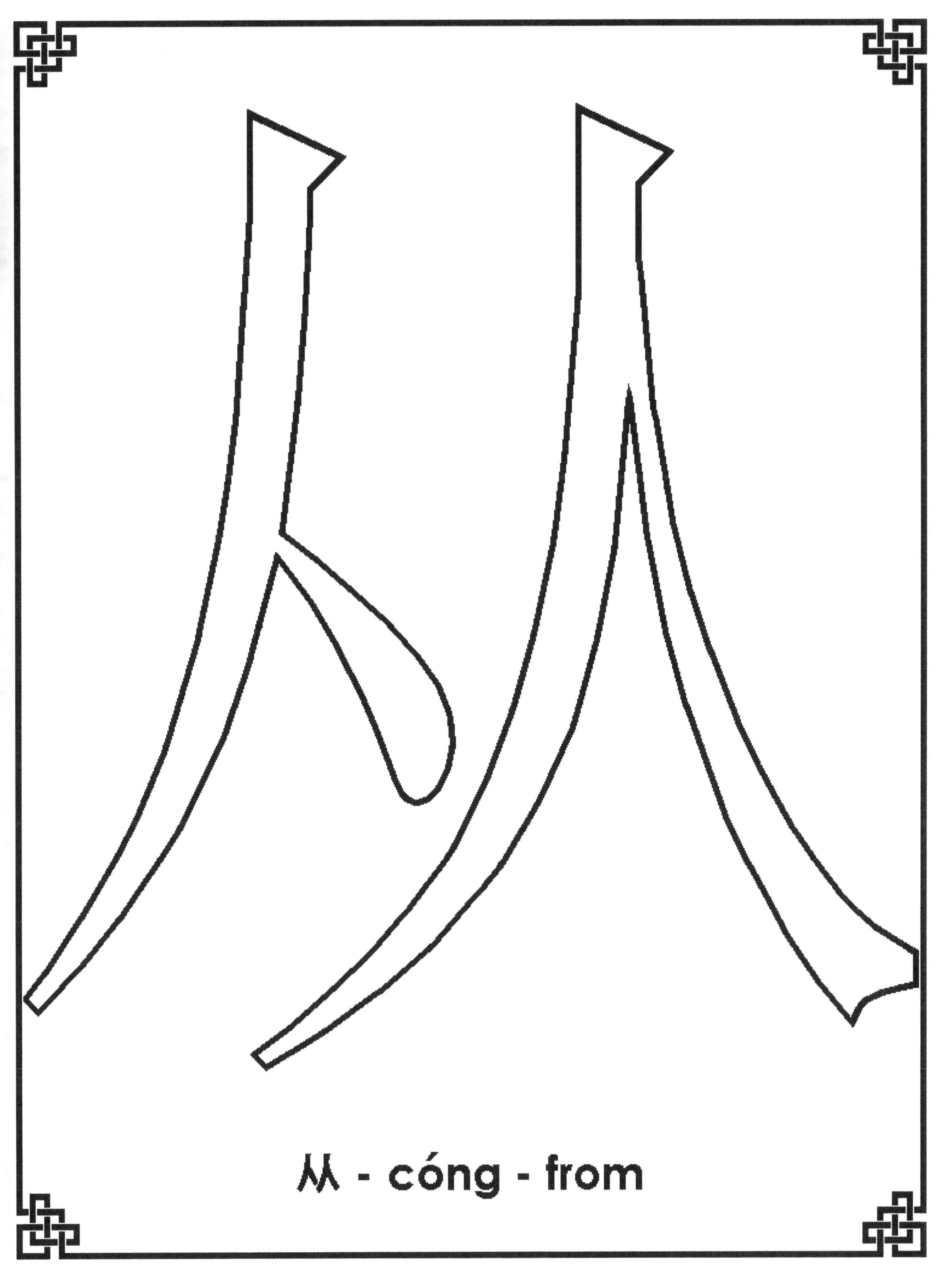

从 - cóng - from

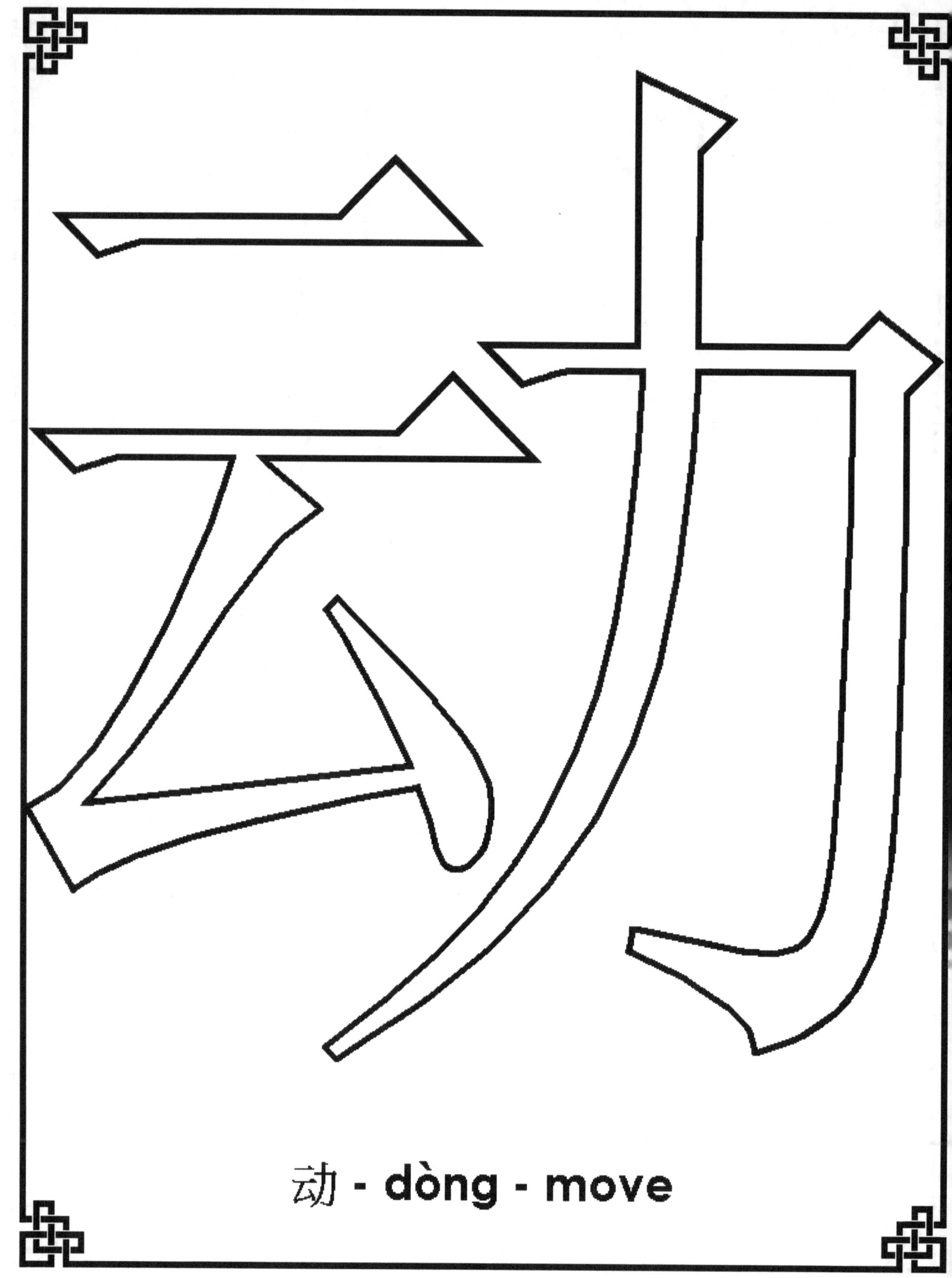

动 - dòng - move

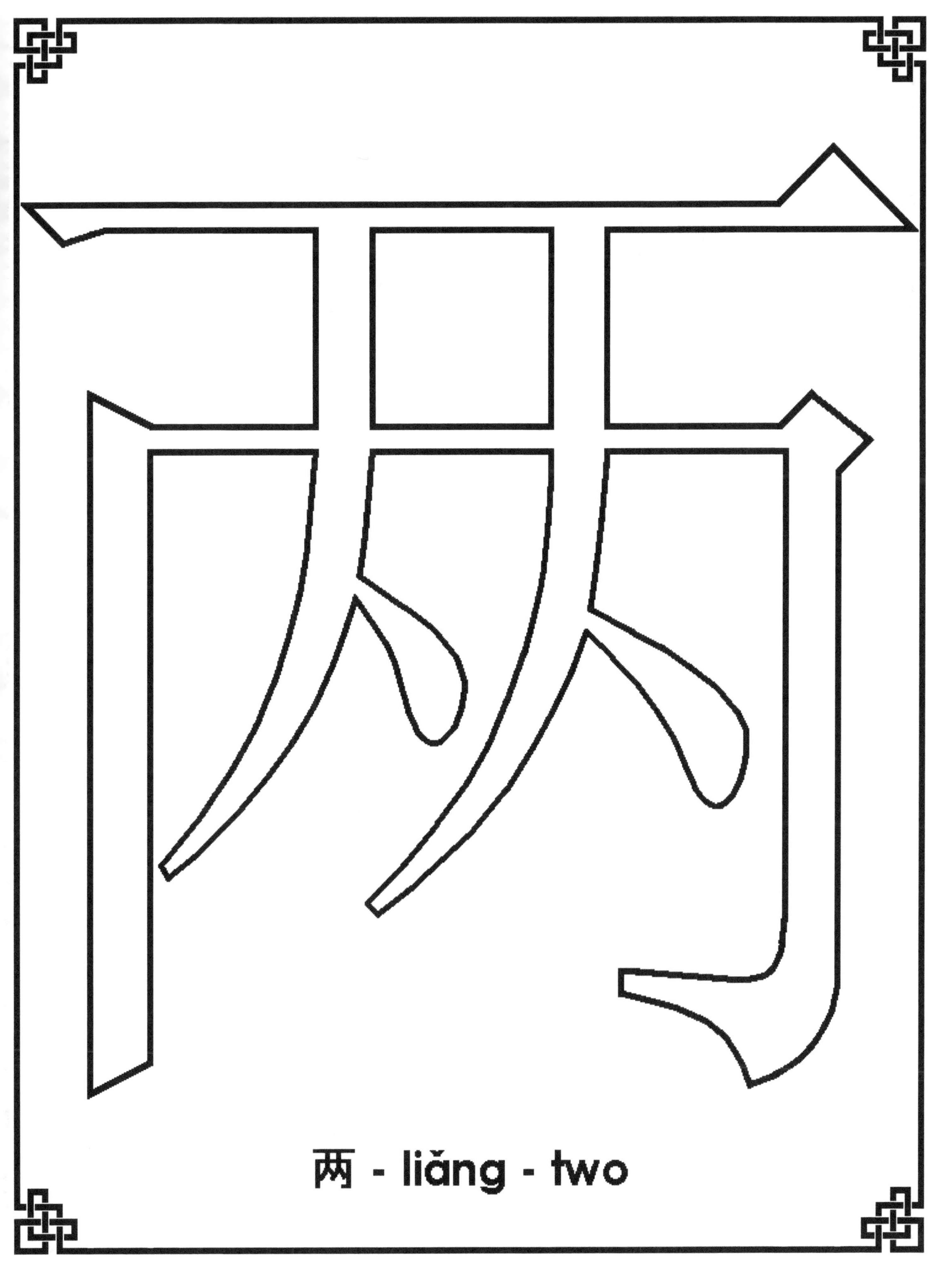

两 - liǎng - two

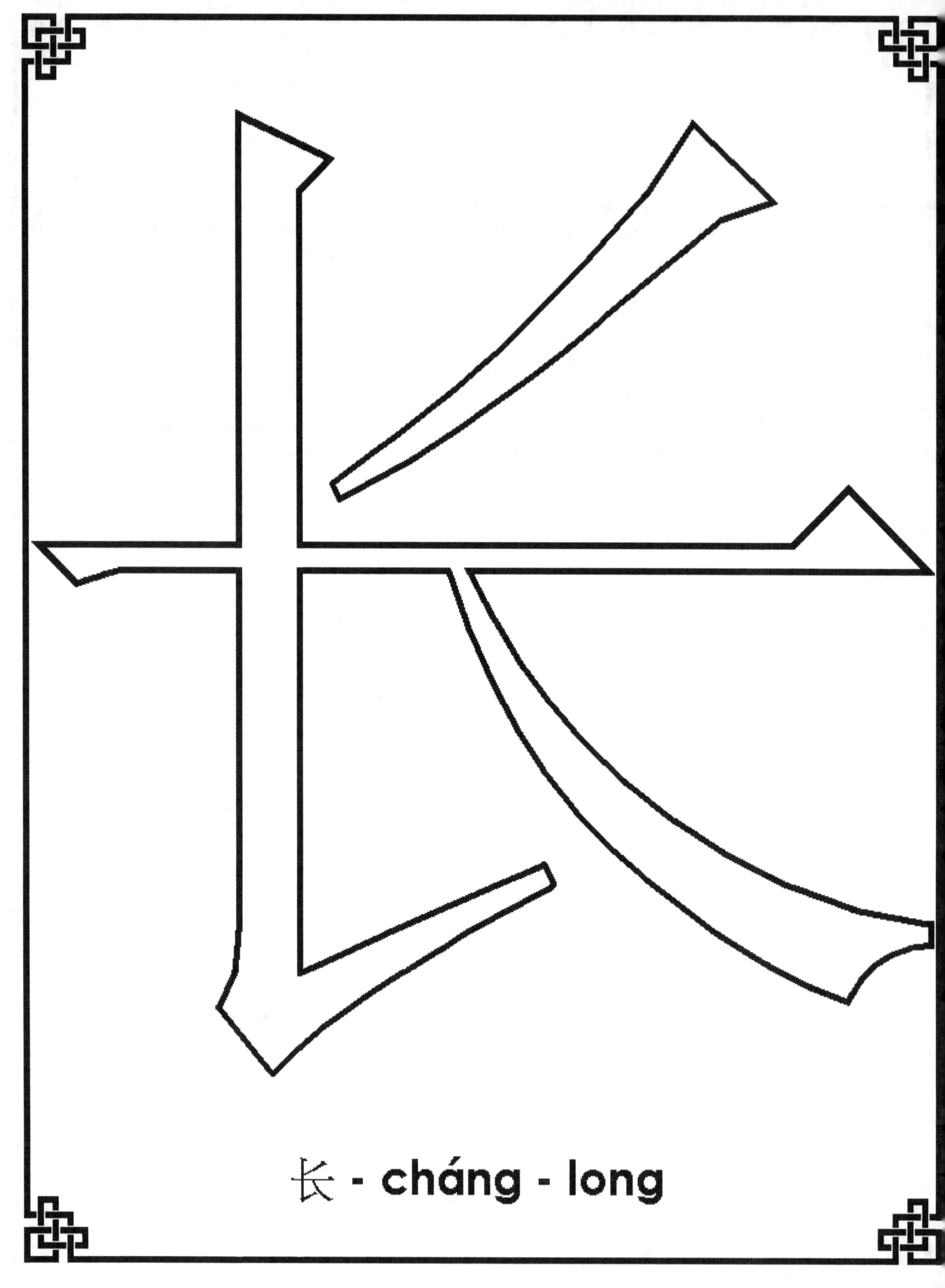

长 - cháng - long